The Algorithmic Mindset

The Algorithmic Mindset

Thinking Like a Machine Without Losing Humanity

Arian Velkor

Mindful Pages

Published in 2026

ISBN: 9789374593240 (PB)
ISBN: 9789374590270 (eBook)

Published by

Mindful Pages
Imprint of Alpha Editions LLC
312 W. 2nd St #1834
Casper, WY 82601, USA

This book was developed using advanced writing tools to support the drafting and ideation process. All content has been thoughtfully curated, refined, and reviewed to ensure quality and relevance.

Content

Introduction viii

Chapter 1 Why We Love Rules (And Break Them) 1

Chapter 2 Define the Real Problem 28

Chapter 3 Build Simple, Robust Algorithms 54

Chapter 4 Data with Dignity 80

Chapter 5 Time, Attention, and Decision Flow 104

Chapter 6 Ethics as a Feature 124

Chapter 7 Teams that Think Clearly 147

Chapter 8 Tools, Not Idols 169

Chapter 9 Personal Algorithms 191

Chapter 10 The Humane Optimiser 213

About the Author 234

Introduction

The story is told quietly in managerial circles, though its consequences were anything but quiet. A well-meaning programmer was asked to optimise a hospital's shift rota. He spent weeks massaging data, learning the subtle differences between night rotations and weekend coverage, modelling the hospital's unpredictable patient flow with admirable diligence. When he unveiled his solution, the results appeared unimpeachable. Costs fell. Overtime evaporated. A tidy dashboard showed clean green indicators across every metric that mattered to the executive team. Yet, within months, nurses were calling in sick at unprecedented rates. Complaints from families rose. A ward that had once run on camaraderie and instinctive mutual support found itself hollowed out by exhaustion. The numbers were right; the care was wrong. Everything that made the hospital humane had slipped through the grid.

This sort of paradox is not confined to hospitals, nor to algorithms. It lives in every workplace that has tried to measure performance and accidentally incentivised the very behaviours that corrode it. It appears in public services designed around throughput rather than dignity. It shows up in households that turn life into a spreadsheet of efficiency, only to find themselves more anxious and less connected. We live among dashboards that promise control and clarity, and yet we continue to make decisions that perplex us. Our systems are cleaner than ever; our lived experience, often messier. The more we optimise, the more something essential seems to leak away.

That tension is the starting point of this book. I have spent years observing the unintended consequences of well-designed rules, the quiet frictions that arise when people try to govern human affairs with the tidy logic of machines. And yet, I have also watched what happens when the pendulum swings in the opposite direction, when instinct reigns unchecked and decisions turn fickle, opaque, and biased. The challenge is not choosing between rules and intuition. It is building a mindset that can use the strengths of both without inheriting their blind spots. We need a way of thinking that borrows the algorithm's precision without surrendering our humanity to its limits.

For centuries, humans have tried to formalise thought. Aristotle carved logic into syllogisms; medieval scholars constructed elaborate decision trees; Enlightenment administrators built bureaucracies grounded in uniform rules. More recently, behavioural science has revealed how often those rules fail under pressure, and how susceptible we are to noise, bias, and fatigue. Meanwhile, modern computer science has given us a language for structure: variables, constraints, thresholds, objective functions. These tools are powerful, but they are also blunt. They illuminate certain truths brilliantly while obscuring others. To think algorithmically is not to replace judgement with code; it is to borrow the clarity of computation while retaining the flexible, empathetic reasoning that machines cannot yet emulate.

This book asks a deceptively simple question: What would it mean to think like a machine without becoming one? To adopt the calm, structured habits of an algorithm while keeping hold of the values and intuitions that make us human? The answer requires more than productivity tips, more than appeals to intuition, and certainly more than blind faith in data. It demands a shift in how we define problems, weigh evidence, and make choices—individually and collectively. It requires humility about our own reasoning and honesty about the limits of automation. And it calls for a deeper understanding of the ethical commitments that must anchor any system capable of affecting human lives.

In the pages that follow, we will build what I call the algorithmic mindset: a disciplined, humane approach to decision-making that blends structure with sensitivity. It is a way of thinking that says, "Let us clarify what we are optimising for," while also asking, "Whom might we harm if we get this wrong?" It recognises that most decisions do not require sophisticated modelling; they require clear objectives, simple heuristics, and transparent checks. It teaches us to define problems in terms precise enough to act on, yet generous enough to honour the complexity of the world. Ultimately, it invites us to treat thinking itself as a craft—one that can be refined through practice.

Consider a recurring metaphor that will surface throughout this book: the truce. A truce is not a merger, nor a surrender. It is an agreement to coexist constructively. Gut instincts operate quickly, drawing on patterns forged through experience. Structured rules operate slowly, demanding consistency and discipline. Left alone, each can cause trouble. Intuition can mislead; rules can ossify. But when held in a careful truce—when intuition initiates a judgement and structure refines it—we approach something robust. A truce is a reminder that different modes of thought need not compete; they can check and complete one another. It is this negotiated balance, rather than any one technique, that underpins the algorithmic mindset.

To understand why this matters now, we must confront a truth that modern life makes painfully clear: our cognitive landscape is overcrowded. We are bombarded with decisions of wildly varying importance, from the trivial to the existential. We face more choices than any previous generation, and we are expected to make them faster, with greater transparency, and under conditions of relentless scrutiny. Our tools have multiplied, yet our attention has not. The result is an environment in which people ricochet between overthinking and underthinking, absorbing vast quantities of information without knowing which fragments to trust. We do not suffer from a lack of data; we suffer from a lack of decision architectures that help us use it well.

History shows that every leap in information technology—from the printing press to the telegraph to the spreadsheet—has required an accompanying leap in cognitive discipline. When new tools increase our ability to measure and record, they also increase the risk of mistaking the measurable for the meaningful. The current wave of machine-assisted decision systems is no different. If we do not develop internal safeguards—principles for interpretation, rules for escalation, habits of ethical reflection—we risk allowing the machinery of optimisation to harden into a worldview. Numbers can help us see; they can also dazzle us into blindness.

The hospital rota incident at the opening of this introduction is not a failure of algorithms. It is a failure of mindset. The programmer built a system that optimised the wrong thing because the organisation failed to articulate what truly mattered. It is easy to mock such mistakes, but we all make them. We pursue speed over clarity, cost over care, convenience over wisdom. We chase quantifiable improvements and overlook the human consequences that do not fit neatly into the model. We confuse the elegance of a solution with its appropriateness. And we forget that every system is shaped by the assumptions that birthed it.

This book is designed to intervene before those errors take hold. Each chapter builds a set of mental tools: a pattern for clarifying goals, a heuristic for selecting variables, a checklist for ethical hazards, a cadence for improving team decisions. These are deliberately lightweight—simple enough to remember under pressure, flexible enough to adapt across contexts. They are not technologies but habits. They create just enough structure to prevent drift without overwhelming your natural judgement. At their best, they make thinking feel less like firefighting and more like stewardship.

But these tools alone will not suffice. A truly algorithmic mindset requires an attentiveness to the texture of human experience: the fragility of trust, the weight of dignity, the comfort of fairness. It demands that we use our computational clarity in service of humane aims. Machines do not feel the consequences of their outputs; we do. A rule that is technically correct may still be devastating in practice. A model that is statistically sound may still undermine the values we claim to uphold. The humane optimiser acknowledges this and builds constraints—ethical, procedural, relational—into every decision.

There is also a personal dimension. Each of us carries implicit algorithms shaped by upbringing, culture, and habit. We follow scripts we barely recognise. We react to certain stimuli with well-rehearsed mental shortcuts. To cultivate the algorithmic mindset is to examine these internal scripts with curiosity rather than defensiveness. It is to ask why certain choices exhaust us while others energise us. It is to design our own internal decision flows—morning systems that clear cognitive fog, evening audits that close mental loops, criteria that help us say no without guilt. In a world overflowing with external algorithms, the most important ones may be the ones we craft for ourselves.

The stakes are high. Organisations that fail to make decisions well become sluggish, mistrusted, or brittle. Teams trapped in cycles of noise and indecision waste talent and morale. Individuals overwhelmed by choice fatigue drift into apathy or impulsiveness. At a societal level, we risk the quiet calcification of public life as more decisions are outsourced to opaque systems with unexamined values. What begins as an efficiency measure can gradually erode our collective capacity for judgement.

Yet the future is not predetermined. We stand at a moment when the boundaries between human and machine reasoning are being actively negotiated. Our tools will continue to evolve, but our responsibility remains constant: to ensure that these tools serve human flourishing rather than replace it. The algorithmic mindset is not an argument for more automation;

it is an argument for more thoughtful humans. It invites us to use computational clarity to illuminate the moral terrain rather than flatten it.

In the chapters ahead, we will ask difficult questions. What happens when a rule that improves consistency inadvertently amplifies bias? How do we design systems that anticipate harm rather than merely react to it? What does it look like to build a team that thinks clearly together? How do we measure success without losing sight of what cannot be measured? And perhaps most importantly, how do we preserve the dignity of people inside systems that are increasingly governed by metrics?

I cannot promise definitive answers to all these questions, because the answers vary across contexts and will continue to evolve. But I can promise a framework—a way of approaching problems with both rigour and generosity. A way of navigating the world's complexity without becoming overwhelmed by it. A way of thinking that clarifies, steadies, and ultimately humanises our decisions.

The algorithmic mindset is within reach. It asks you to slow down long enough to define what truly matters, then speed up again with purpose. It asks you to design your own guardrails rather than inherit someone else's. It asks you to hold precision and compassion in the same mental space. Above all, it asks you to remember that every rule is a choice, every model a story, every metric a judgement about what is worth counting.

The pages ahead invite you into this practice. The work is demanding but liberating. If we get it right, our dashboards may still be tidy, but our lives—and the lives of those shaped by our decisions—will be richer, fairer, and unmistakably more human.

Chapter 1
Why We Love Rules (And Break Them)

Rules enter our lives quietly. They rarely announce themselves as such; instead, they appear as habits, traditions, shortcuts, and "the way things are done around here". Consider a small vignette from a mid-sized technology company. A hiring manager, overwhelmed by a flood of applications, uses a quick rule of thumb: shortlist anyone who has worked at two brand-name firms and ignore the rest. It is efficient—astonishingly so. Within minutes, a pile of hundreds becomes a neat row of five. Yet when the team later reflects on persistent sameness in their hires, no-one remembers this filter. The rule had been intuitive, almost invisible, but its effects were enduring. It saved time, but at a cost they had never fully examined.

This quiet tension—between the clarity rules offer and the blind spots they smuggle in—is the heartbeat of modern decision-making. We claim to value nuance, but we are drawn to simplicity. We praise careful deliberation, but under pressure we reach for fast judgements. The contradiction is not hypocrisy; it is human nature grappling with cognitive scarcity. Our attention is limited, our time is fragmented, and our world is too complex to analyse everything from first principles. Rules step in as the mind's first line of defence. And yet, as the earlier hiring example suggests, their speed can conceal their distortions.

Our ancestors were no different. The earliest legal codes, inscribed on clay tablets, were attempts to reduce the chaos of human life to a manageable set of "if–then" directives. Hunters tracking game made instant decisions based on patterns passed down orally. Sailors navigating by stars followed sequences learned through repetition rather than calculation. These weren't primitive workarounds. They were elegant adaptations to environments where slow thinking was dangerous, even fatal. The appeal of rules is ancient; so too are their limitations. What has changed is not our psychology but the magnitude of decisions we now try to compress into these mental shortcuts.

This chapter explores why rules exert such magnetic pull on the human mind, why we cling to them even after they fail us, and how we might use them with greater intelligence. To understand this, we must begin with our dependence on heuristics—those quick, frugal mental models that guide most of what we do. We like to imagine ourselves as careful analysts, weighing the evidence with judicial calm. Yet behavioural research shows that much of our thinking is patterned and habitual, relying on cognitive shortcuts designed to conserve energy. These heuristics are not lazy; they are efficient. They free us to focus on what truly matters. But they come with liabilities: they can smuggle bias past our scrutiny; they can lure us into overconfidence; they can amplify inequalities without anyone actively wishing for such outcomes.

Take again the hiring manager. His heuristic was not arbitrary. It was based on experience: candidates from certain firms had historically performed well. In contexts of overload, this shortcut can outperform more elaborate scoring mechanisms. But left unexamined, it privileges the already privileged and erases unconventional talent. This is one of the central themes of the chapter: rules that work well operationally can be ethically troubling, and only by inspecting them do we see the full picture.

The problem, however, is not merely bias. It is noise: the random variation in human judgement that plagues decisions across domains. Two managers evaluating the same candidate often diverge wildly. Doctors reading identical scans disagree on diagnoses. Judges vary in sentencing not because of evidence but because of mood, timing, or sheer cognitive drift. Noise is insidious. Bias at least has direction; noise is arbitrary.

It wastes money, corrodes trust, and erodes fairness. One of this chapter's ambitions is to show how rules—used selectively—can reduce noise without constricting good judgement. A simple pattern, *normalise, then decide*, can make a remarkable difference. Before making a decision, align your criteria, ensure that everyone is judging along the same dimensions, and only then deliberate. It is a modest intervention with disproportionate benefits.

In the world of performance reviews, noise is especially destructive. A team might believe it is operating a fair system, yet the variability between reviewers can turn promotions into a lottery. What seems like personal discretion often masks systematic inconsistency. When organisations introduce shared scoring rubrics—not rigidly as a bureaucratic straightjacket, but as a shared vocabulary—noise drops sharply. People begin to calibrate themselves. Conversations become more grounded. Disagreements still occur, but they occur above a firmer foundation. Throughout this chapter, we will examine how small structural nudges can align our instincts with our intentions.

But the story of rule-making would be incomplete if we treated rules as the hero. There are contexts where intuition outperforms analysis, where experts develop a fluency that no checklist can match. The trick is recognising the signs. Intuition excels in stable domains with rapid, reliable feedback. A paramedic arriving at the scene of an accident does not compose a mental spreadsheet. She draws upon thousands of hours of pattern recognition. The tiniest details—a patient's posture, skin tone, breathing cadence—trigger a cascade of internal assessments. This is not "gut feeling" in the mystical sense. It is compressed knowledge, trained through exposure and honed through repetition.

Yet intuition misfires in unstable or deceptive environments. Without consistent feedback, we learn the wrong lessons. We grow confident in patterns that do not exist or cling to habits formed under outdated conditions. A major thread running through this chapter is the importance of distinguishing when to trust intuition and when to structure it. We will explore a set of practical signals that indicate when intuitive judgement deserves deference and when it requires reinforcement.

Between rule and instinct lies what may be the most fruitful territory: the truce. A truce is not harmony. It is negotiated coexistence. It asks gut feeling to offer the first impression and structured thinking to provide the second pass. This two-stage flow, developed further in the chapter, is deceptively simple: scan intuitively, then review deliberately. The scan gives you speed; the review gives you stability. If both align, proceed. If they diverge, slow down, interrogate the conflict, and escalate if necessary.

In practice, this approach can transform decision-making. Imagine a leadership meeting where a thorny choice—say, whether to approve a risky project—is on the table. Everyone begins with an intuitive read: *Does this feel promising or hazardous? Why?* These impressions are captured without debate. Only after each person has articulated their first response are structured criteria applied. Feasibility, cost, strategic alignment, downside risk: the grid brings order. When intuition and structure converge, decisions become swift and confident. When they clash, the disagreement becomes visible and can be examined without ego. This truce is not only efficient; it is respectful. It acknowledges that our fast-thinking self has valuable insights but that those insights deserve to be tested.

Why does any of this matter now? Because the pressures that overwhelm modern decision-making are intensifying. Information overload, tighter deadlines, greater scrutiny, and the ascendancy of metrics all converge on the individual professional, who is expected to think clearly in conditions that punish clarity. Rules become seductive because they reduce cognitive load. Yet they are dangerous if followed blindly. Intuition becomes seductive because it feels natural. Yet it is dangerous if trusted universally. This chapter offers a framework for navigating this duality with maturity.

The stakes extend beyond workplaces. Our political judgements, our personal relationships, our consumption habits—all are shaped by rules and instincts we barely recognise. Understanding them is not an abstract exercise; it is a way of reclaiming agency. It allows us to see the architecture of our own thought and to redesign it where necessary.

As you move through this chapter, you will encounter tools that help you separate helpful patterns from harmful ones. You will learn why randomness in judgement is far more costly than most organisations appreciate, and how small shifts can create disproportionate improvements. You will see how experts in high-stakes environments cultivate intuition responsibly and why novices often overestimate theirs. And you will explore the idea of the truce—a recurring motif throughout the book—where gut and grid collaborate rather than compete.

These pages will not ask you to abandon your instincts, nor will they ask you to submit unquestioningly to structure. Instead, they invite you to understand your own mind more deeply, to recognise the mechanics beneath your judgements, and to refine them with care. If the book's introduction presented the tension between algorithmic precision and human judgement, this chapter takes you into the first chamber of that tension: the rules we love, the rules we resist, and the rules we quietly obey without noticing.

By the time you finish, I hope you will see rules not as constraints but as instruments—tools that, when tuned properly, can amplify your best thinking and dampen your cognitive noise. And I hope you will recognise when it is time to put the rulebook aside and trust a well-trained intuition instead. The path between these modes of thought is not always clear, but learning to navigate it is one of the most liberating skills a decision-maker can acquire.

Heuristics, Biases, and Helpful Shortcuts

In March 2015, at Google's Mountain View campus, Laszlo Bock's People Operations team confronted a puzzle. Two engineering managers, reviewing the same candidate's file on the same afternoon, produced sharply different assessments. One argued the applicant was "top one per cent". The other judged the same portfolio "borderline". Both had decades of experience. Both followed the company's formal rubric. The divergence could not be chalked up to expertise or mood alone. It was a reminder, documented later in Bock's *Work Rules!* (2015), that even in a data-rich environment staffed by analytical thinkers, human judgement drifts. It bends with context, attention, and the quiet shortcuts the mind takes to preserve energy. That drift is costly. It shapes hiring lists, performance reviews, and the trajectories of entire teams. And it is why heuristics—those fast, frugal rules of thumb—sit at the centre of every consequential decision we make. They are efficient. They also carry risk. They demand respect, but they require scrutiny.

The scene at Google is ordinary in one sense: every professional environment depends on heuristics to keep work moving. When a manager screens applications, when a committee triages grant proposals, when a doctor weighs symptoms, the mind compresses information at speed. The compression is not a flaw. It is a solution to scarcity: scarce time, scarce attention, scarce cognitive bandwidth. A well-chosen heuristic can outperform slower analysis because it reduces noise—the random, unpredictable misalignment between two people assessing the same case. Yet the same shortcut can amplify bias when its underlying pattern reflects a narrow slice of experience. A shortlist rule, applied unquestioningly, becomes a gate rather than a guide. This is the tension running through this section: heuristics help us navigate complexity, but they can mislead without counterweights.

Consider a hiring example that has become emblematic in organisational psychology. In London in 2018, a fintech firm facing aggressive growth targets adopted a quick heuristic to accelerate its recruitment pipeline. Any applicant who had completed a two-year stint at a major North American technology company was automatically fast-tracked to interview. The logic was simple: those firms were known to run demanding selection processes and structured training programmes. The heuristic halved screening time. It correlated, for a while, with strong performance. But as the firm reviewed its data two years later, a pattern surfaced. Candidates who had graduated from local universities or had worked in smaller European startups were dramatically underrepresented—not because they lacked skill, but because they lacked the specific brand markers the heuristic prized. What began as a practical shortcut quietly hardened into a structural bias. The speed was real. The cost was hidden.

The mechanics of this effect are well-established. Show the behaviour first: a manager moves through a hundred CVs and notices familiar logos. Name the mechanism: availability bias, documented by Tversky and Kahneman (1973), where the mind overweights information that comes to it easily. Explain the consequence: the heuristic conflates familiarity with quality, nudging the manager to favour candidates who "look" successful rather than those whose achievements align with the job's demands. The implication is sobering. Even when a heuristic starts as a benign time-saver, it can encode assumptions that, left unchallenged, shape the texture of a workforce.

Yet heuristics are not inherently problematic. In fact, much research suggests they can outperform complex models when the environment is noisy or the inputs unreliable. Gerd

Gigerenzer's work at the Max Planck Institute (2007) shows that simple decision rules often yield superior predictions because they avoid overfitting—our tendency to tune analysis too closely to past data. A rules-of-thumb approach can preserve generality when precision is both illusory and expensive. The hiring manager who uses a "shortlist three candidates from three distinct backgrounds" heuristic may produce richer, more creative teams than a colleague who builds an elaborate scoring spreadsheet with twenty variables. Here the motif of the *filter* becomes useful. A filter shapes light; it does not create it. A heuristic filters complexity. The skill lies in choosing the filter consciously rather than inheriting it unconsciously.

To see this from another angle, look at a context where heuristics excel. In 1976, at St George's Hospital in Tooting, London, research documented how experienced nurses made near-instant triage decisions in the emergency department. Their assessments often anticipated doctors' later diagnoses, not because they were analysing faster, but because they were noticing patterns—skin tone, breathing shallow or deep, micro-delays in response. These visual and auditory cues, embedded through repeated exposure, formed a kind of compressed knowledge. The domain was stable, the feedback rapid, and the stakes immediate. Intuition thrived under these conditions. The heuristic was not "trust your gut" but "trust the patterns encoded through years of close contact with real patients". A machine-learning researcher might call it a model trained on high-quality labelled data. A clinician would call it experience.

But even in domains where heuristics shine, there are limitations. The counter-example is instructive. In 2013, the National Audit Office reviewed diagnostic delays across several NHS trusts and found that rapid triage occasionally misclassified atypical cases—heart attacks presenting without chest pain, strokes manifesting with subtle facial changes. These were rare, but the rarity mattered. A heuristic shaped by common cases can miss the edge cases. Reconciling this tension reveals the heart of the challenge. A heuristic is only as reliable as the environment in which it was formed. When that environment shifts or when variability increases, the shortcut begins to wobble.

The same instability appears in corporate life. A hiring manager may rely on a heuristic formed ten years earlier in a different labour market. The behaviour is visible: scanning CVs for the same degree programmes or work histories that once predicted performance. The explanation is ecological rationality: the heuristic suited one environment but not another. The implication is a call for periodic recalibration. Without it, the filter distorts more than it clarifies.

Noise is the second force shaping this landscape. Daniel Kahneman, Olivier Sibony, and Cass Sunstein's *Noise* (2021) quantified the degree to which similar professionals disagree without reason. When Chicago court judges sentenced identical hypothetical cases in 2013, the variability spanned months, not days. When insurance underwriters in New York evaluated the same claim in 2016, their assessments varied by thousands of dollars. These are not differences of opinion. They are noise—randomness masquerading as judgement. And heuristics interact with noise in intricate ways. A good heuristic reduces the space for drift. A bad one magnifies it.

To manage noise, organisations increasingly adopt normalisation steps. In 2019, a British civil service department piloted a system where reviewers scored candidate evidence individually, then compared differences before forming a collective judgement. The behaviour was small: reviewers met for ten minutes to look at discrepancies. The explanation was clear: aligning criteria reduces random variance. The implication was significant. The department reported steadier hiring patterns and fewer contested decisions. A simple "normalise, then decide" flow nudged individuals away from idiosyncratic readings and toward shared interpretation.

This does not remove bias, but it shapes how heuristics operate. A manager using a shortlist heuristic after a normalisation step is making a different kind of choice from one using the same shortcut without calibration. One is filtering with awareness; the other is filtering blindly. The motif of the filter returns here: every decision passes through a lens. The question is whether that lens has been cleaned.

Where heuristics misfire, the costs accrue silently. A firm might notice that its leadership pipeline lacks diversity, but the source of the distortion could be a filtering rule applied two levels earlier: favour candidates who switch roles every eighteen months, or prioritise those who have managed teams of a certain size. Such rules reward specific career paths and penalise others. The rule seems neutral. The metric appears objective. But the behaviour it rewards—frequent role changes—may reflect differences in financial security or prior access to mentorship. The heuristic shapes opportunity long before anyone realises it.

However, focusing solely on bias gives an incomplete picture. There is also the danger of overanalysis. In 2009, the UK's Local Government Association reported that some councils reviewing procurement bids had introduced scoring algorithms with dozens of weighted factors. These models aimed to increase fairness. Instead, they created procedural inertia: small differences in input data, often uncertain, produced artificially precise rankings. Staff described the process as "numbers pretending to be judgement". Here, the heuristic "choose the top-scoring vendor" misfired because the underlying model was too complex for the available evidence. The filter was opaque. The implication is counterintuitive but essential: when uncertainty is high, simpler heuristics can improve consistency because they limit the false certainty complex models impose.

This leads to a deeper question: where do heuristics gain their authority? They gain it from stories—narratives about what has worked before. A hiring heuristic is a story about past success. A diagnostic heuristic is a story about patterns learned on the job. When the story is accurate and the domain stable, the shortcut is powerful. When the story is outdated, incomplete, or biased, the shortcut becomes a liability. The trick is not to abandon heuristics but to examine their origin. A good heuristic is neither sacred nor disposable. It is conditional.

For professionals who operate under constant pressure, this can feel like an exhausting demand. Yet the practice need not be complicated. The first step is to surface the heuristic explicitly. What rule am I following? What pattern am I privileging? The behaviour of naming the rule changes its power. A manager who says aloud, "I tend to prioritise candidates from these institutions because historically they've performed well," gains a vantage point for assessment. That vantage point reveals alternatives: performance may correlate with training quality, but training quality appears in many places. By articulating the heuristic, the manager can design a counterweight—review one candidate from a different background, or introduce a normalisation step before shortlisting. The filter becomes visible. And once visible, it can be adjusted.

Heuristics also intersect with emotion. Professionals often recall vivid failures more intensely than mundane successes. This colours the shortcuts they adopt. A researcher who once hired a brilliant generalist may overgeneralise that pattern; another who faced trouble with a similarly profiled candidate may discard the category entirely. This is affective bias. It alters the filter without announcing the change. The implication is subtle: when emotional memory drives heuristics, recalibration must include periods of emotional distance, or the rule becomes a proxy for a single salient event rather than a broad pattern.

What, then, should the reader carry forward? Not a toolkit, nor a prescription, but a question. Each heuristic contains a claim about the world. Some of those claims hold. Others decay. The challenge is to inspect the filter without discarding the light. To ask, when making the next shortlist, or assessment, or rapid judgement: *What rule am I following, and what would happen if I softened it?* The tension remains unresolved, but productive. A shortcut saves time; a misapplied shortcut shapes lives. The test is simple, and it lingers: *Is this rule helping me see, or is it keeping something important out of view?*

The Cost of Cognitive Noise

In February 2013, at Cook County Court in Chicago, a research team observing sentencing patterns noticed something unsettling. Two judges, examining identical hypothetical cases on the same morning, diverged by months in the sentences they assigned. One recommended probation. Another insisted on custodial time. The judges were not inexperienced. They were not pressed for time. Yet their decisions—documented that year in a study later cited by Kahneman, Sibony, and Sunstein (2021)—varied so dramatically that chance seemed to play as much of a role as law. The randomness was not malicious. It was noise: the invisible scatter that creeps into human judgement, widening gaps that no rulebook intends. A human system, running smoothly on the surface, leaked fairness through its seams. The sight was disturbing because it was ordinary.

Noise thrives in the quiet moments of judgement: the glance at a performance form, the hesitation before marking a score, the seconds in which fatigue or mood nudge a number upwards or downwards. At a London insurance firm in 2016, later profiled in *Noise*, underwriters assessing the same claim produced valuations differing by thousands of pounds. The organisation assumed its processes delivered consistency. The data told another story. Variability had crept in unnoticed, the way a draft enters a house through a loose window. The motif of the *draft* matters here. Noise is rarely loud. It slips through gaps no-one remembers opening.

Show the behaviour: managers filling performance review templates in December, eyes tired, minds full, marking a "4" instead of a "3" because the difference feels minor. Name the mechanism: cognitive noise—a pattern of unpredictable, directionless variation across people evaluating identical material. Explain the consequence: decisions drift without reason, producing outcomes dependent on who happens to be holding the pen. The implication is stark. An organisation may pride itself on fairness and still allow randomness to shape careers.

This quiet drift is distinct from bias. Bias has direction: it pushes judgement systematically towards certain groups or patterns. Noise has none. It is scatter. Its presence often remains invisible until someone measures it. That invisibility makes it dangerous, especially in processes with consequences for pay, promotion, or public trust. A minor rating discrepancy at an annual review can accumulate into meaningful salary differences over several cycles. A hiring panel's inconsistent scoring can turn recruitment into chance. A prosecutor's variable risk assessment can shape lives in ways they cannot see.

Consider a verifiable example. In 2018, the UK Civil Service Commission audited several departments' performance review systems across London and Bristol. They compared how different managers rated identical anonymised profiles. Even after official training, variation remained high: one department's managers ranged from "needs improvement" to "exceeds expectations" for the same profile. The show element was clear: identical work histories, different ratings. Naming the mechanism—noise—enabled the next step. The explanation emerged: criteria, though written, had not been interpreted uniformly. The implication was practical: no amount of policy writing could compensate for inconsistent interpretation by individual reviewers.

The counter-example tells us a little more. In 2001, the Royal College of Surgeons reviewed surgical training assessments across five UK hospitals. Variation was surprisingly low. Trainees rated by different consultants received near-identical scores. The environment was structured; the criteria granular; the behaviours observable. This stands as a limit case. Noise is not inevitable. Under certain conditions—clear standards, shared training, repeated exposure—it can shrink dramatically. The reconciliation lies in the domain. Surgery training uses behavioural anchors and highly specific thresholds; performance reviews in many offices rely on holistic impressions. The draft enters where the frame is loose.

Noise also erodes trust. Trust is not an abstraction here; it appears in visible reactions. Employees compare their ratings with colleagues and spot discrepancies unexplained by performance. The metric of "perceived fairness", captured in engagement surveys, slides. People commit less energy to systems they see as arbitrary. When randomness becomes the hidden influencer of outcomes, the entire structure begins to wobble. The draft rattles more loudly.

To counter this drift, some organisations use normalisation. The principle is simple: before deciding, align interpretations. In March 2019, a major UK government agency piloted a calibration step for performance reviews across its Manchester offices. Reviewers scored employees individually. Then, in short sessions, they compared discrepancies, explaining why one had marked a "3" and another a "5". The behaviour seems modest—ten-minute huddles rather than long meetings. Naming it—normalisation—gives it structure. The explanation is straightforward: shared discussion nudged individuals towards common standards. The implication was immediate. Noise narrowed. The agency found fewer outliers and fewer contested results.

Normalisation does not eliminate judgement. It synchronises it. Consider the motif of the draft again. By sealing small gaps—clarifying criteria, aligning interpretations—you reduce airflow. The structure remains flexible, but the drift tightens. What emerges is not uniformity but coherence. A manager still exercises discretion, but that discretion operates within a shared frame.

Noise also interacts with context. A manager completing reviews after a twelve-hour week makes different micro-decisions from one who reviews in fresh conditions. Kahneman et al. (2021) cite research showing that judges in Israel in 2011 were more likely to deny parole before lunch. The show element is explicit: decision patterns changed with hunger. Naming the mechanism drifts into physiological noise: bodily states seep into judgement. The explanation, while uncomfortable, is simple: without protective processes, humans leak variability. The implication matters for professional environments. Without structural safeguards, even conscientious individuals produce randomness.

Yet we must consider a limit case again. In 2014, the Metropolitan Police introduced a structured review system for officer promotion interviews. It included anchored scoring guides, independent assessors, and a rotation system. Subsequent audits in 2016 found noise significantly reduced. This does not mean intuition plays no role. It means the system reduced the influence of irrelevant variation—mood, fatigue, or unspoken heuristics. Reconciling the counter-example shows the path forward. Noise is not destiny. It is design.

Now return to performance reviews. A manager, confronted with a list of twelve employees, begins by marking the most recent projects because they are prominent in memory. The behaviour is recency bias layered with noise. Naming the dynamic exposes the interaction. The explanation: without calibration, the manager's ratings depend partly on what happens to be top of mind. The implication: outcomes shift unpredictably, and employees notice.

Introduce a normalise-then-decide pattern and the scene changes. Reviewers first list the criteria they believe matter—impact, reliability, collaboration—and compare with colleagues to create shared definitions. They then assess individuals. Finally, they reconvene to examine score spreads: Why did one person receive a higher collaboration score? Which evidence supports that? This pattern does not suppress individuality. It channels it. Each reviewer still commits to a score, but noise is constrained.

At a global bank's London office in 2020, this pattern turned a chaotic mid-year review cycle into a steadier one. Managers reported that discussions became less about personal impressions and more about evidence, prompting small course corrections in scores. Variability shrank. When surveyed six months later, employees reported greater trust in the process—not because scores were higher, but because they were clearer. Trust appeared in behaviour: employees prepared review documents with more specificity, expecting their work to be assessed consistently. The draft grew weaker.

But limits remain. Normalisation cannot fully account for ambiguous evidence. In creative roles, for instance, output may defy easy measurement. In January 2022, a media organisation in London attempted to normalise its editorial performance assessments. Reviewers found that some qualitative attributes resisted shared thresholds. The counter-example is valuable. Not all domains respond equally to structure. Yet even in these contexts, the act of naming disagreements exposes hidden drifts. Reconciliation comes from acknowledging that some noise is tolerable when creativity is valued, provided the process remains transparent. The window stays open by choice, not neglect.

Noise has financial consequences. When underwriters' valuations vary by thousands of pounds, premiums fluctuate unpredictably. When performance ratings drift, compensation becomes uneven. When procurement committees diverge, vendor selection becomes erratic. Each deviation produces a measurable cost. Not a metaphorical one—a budgetary one. It appears in spreadsheets as variance unexplained by strategy.

Noise also shapes organisational memory. Decisions scattered in every direction produce patterns difficult to learn from. A team cannot refine its approach if randomness blurs its signals. The motif of the draft surfaces again. A gust here, a gust there, and soon the building feels colder. Noise chills learning.

The deepest cost is moral. When randomness influences outcomes, a quiet unfairness sets in. People feel it before they articulate it. A colleague receives a strong rating on thin evidence; another receives a middling one despite consistent effort. The organisation's narrative—"We evaluate fairly"—pulls against lived experience. This tension corrodes. And once trust cracks, no amount of policy rewriting repairs it quickly.

So the unresolved question lingers. At the next review cycle, when a manager sits before a form and hesitates between two scores, will the decision reflect evidence or drift? Will the process have sealed its windows, or will the draft return? The choice lies not only in methods but in attention. The test is simple, but demanding: *What part of this judgement is mine, and what part might be noise?*

When Intuition Beats Calculation

At 08:14 on 12 June 2017, paramedic Sarah McLoughlin stepped out of an ambulance outside Manchester's Deansgate and walked towards a cyclist who had collided with a delivery van. The scene looked ordinary: a young man sitting upright, answering questions, reassuring bystanders. Yet McLoughlin, who had worked for North West Ambulance Service since 2006, paused. His breathing was too shallow. His responses carried a fractional delay. His skin tone, under the street's early light, held a greyish tint she had seen only in patients masking internal bleeding. Within minutes she activated a "red" call, fast-tracking him to Manchester Royal Infirmary. A CT scan confirmed a splenic rupture. The decision, made in seconds, almost certainly saved his life. No calculation could have produced it at that speed. The judgement arose from pattern recognition—years of sensory exposure compressed into rapid inference.

That scene captures a truth professionals in stable, high-feedback domains know intimately: intuition can beat analysis when the environment teaches swiftly and reliably. It is not magic. It is not guesswork. It is accumulated structure. And it looks ordinary until it isn't. The motif of the *glance* runs through this section—the brief moment in which observation crystallises into action. McLoughlin's glance was trained, not mystical. It emerged from repeated experience of how real injuries present differently from textbook cases.

To understand where intuition excels, we must show its mechanics before we name them. Watch an experienced paramedic move through a scene: the quick scan of posture, the tracking of breath, the count of seconds between responses. These behaviours create near-instant triage. Name the mechanism: recognition-primed decision-making, described by Gary Klein in *Sources of Power* (1998), in which experts match the structure of a situation to stored patterns. Explain the engine: the domain feeds rapid, unambiguous feedback—was the decision right or wrong?—allowing the expert to refine thousands of micro-patterns. The implication is profound. In certain contexts, the fastest route to accuracy is not computation but fluency.

Stable domains with fast feedback produce this fluency. Emergency medicine, competitive chess, aviation landing checks, and high-volume call centres all offer repeated exposure to similar structures. In each setting, the expert's nervous system updates continuously. Consider a second example. In January 2012 at Heathrow Airport, British Airways captain Mark Vanhoenacker described in a training log how senior pilots could detect subtle crosswinds during approach long before instruments signalled them. They adjusted throttle and rudder almost unconsciously. The behaviour was small: a slight shift in pressure on the control column. Naming the process revealed its basis: sensorimotor learning shaped through thousands of landings in similar conditions. The explanation was ecological. The cockpit provides immediate feedback. The implication is simple. Where feedback is rapid, intuition sharpens.

Yet the story has limits. A counter-example matters. During the 2008 financial crisis, traders at several London banks relied on intuition formed in comparatively stable pre-crisis markets. Their instincts, once profitable, misread the volatility that followed. The environment had changed. Feedback became noisy, inconsistent, and slow. Intuition decayed. The reconciliation is instructive. Intuition thrives only when the structure of the world remains stable enough to teach. When volatility spikes or when conditions shift faster than experience can update, intuition falters. This is not a weakness of experts; it is a mismatch between pattern and environment.

Returning to environments where intuition does thrive clarifies its distinct character. In emergency care, cues emerge in clusters. In aviation, weather patterns follow seasonal rhythms. In chess, the board's logic is unchanging. These domains reward those who absorb patterns through exposure. Metrics reinforce this: reduced time-to-decision, increased diagnostic accuracy, more stable error rates. Consider how paramedics measure success. Response times, triage accuracy, and avoidable escalations form a feedback loop. Each incident acts as a data point. Over years, these data points shape an internal model far more intricate than any formal checklist.

Show another behaviour: a senior manager in an operations centre glances at a dashboard and senses something misaligned before metrics show red. Name it: tacit knowledge. Explain it: repeated exposure to the organisation's rhythms allows anomalies to stand out. The implication is practical. Attempts to replace such judgement entirely with rules often underperform because rules cannot encode every nuance of a stable domain.

Still, intuition can misfire even in such domains if professionals drift away from feedback. A study from the National Institute for Health Research (NIHR) in 2015 found that clinicians who moved into more managerial roles, reducing patient contact, experienced a decline in diagnostic intuition after several years. The explanation was feedback starvation. Without regular correction, the pattern library stagnated. The implication is important. Intuition must be fed.

This is where practice loops matter. They are not training drills. They are deliberate cycles in which experts revisit outcomes, compare expectations with results, and adjust their mental models. In 2019, the London Ambulance Service introduced short debrief sessions after major incidents. These were not moral evaluations but calibration exercises. Paramedics compared initial triage impressions with eventual diagnoses. The behaviour anchored intuition to reality. The motif of the glance reappears here: the glance becomes sharper when paired with reflection.

Calls for intuition can invite scepticism, particularly in professions obsessed with quantification. Yet intuition does not oppose evidence; it compresses it. In February 2014, a study at University College London measured diagnostic times among radiologists. Experienced radiologists identified abnormalities significantly faster than junior colleagues. Eye-tracking technology revealed that experts fixated on relevant regions almost immediately. Their intuition was visible in their gaze. Name the underlying principle: structure recognition. Explain the implication: intuition externalises knowledge that is too complex to articulate. It is not antithetical to science. It is a product of it.

The limitation, again, deserves scrutiny. When stable domains shift or when rare anomalies break established patterns, intuition can lead experts astray. Aviation offers a sharp reminder. The Air France Flight 447 crash in June 2009, analysed in the BEA report (2012), involved pilots whose intuition—trained in normal flight conditions—misread instrument failures at high altitude. Their internal pattern library contained no analogue for the situation. The implication is chilling but essential. Intuition must be bounded by systems designed to catch rare, catastrophic deviations.

So how do we identify when intuition deserves deference? Look for signals. The first is pattern density: situations repeat with enough similarity to teach. The second is feedback speed: outcomes become clear quickly enough for learning. The third is error cost: mistakes occur often enough to refine judgement without catastrophic loss. Paramedic triage meets all three. The environment is structured. The feedback is rapid. Errors are visible. In these contexts, intuition does not merely supplement rules; it outperforms them.

But the question deepens. What should professionals do when they suspect their domain is stable enough for intuition but fear its limits? The practice loop offers the answer. Commitment to reflection—regular, structured, brief—helps calibrate judgement. The London Ambulance Service's debriefs show the behaviour clearly: ten-minute reviews fuel expertise. The implication spreads beyond emergency medicine. In software engineering, code reviews act as practice loops. In journalism, editorial post-mortems do the same. In each case, intuition is sharpened by structured reflection.

When intuition and analysis collide, the tension reveals something about the domain itself. If the domain is stable, intuition may be signalling information the model cannot capture. If the domain is unstable, the model may be guarding against outdated patterns. The motif of the glance appears once more. The question is whether the glance is grounded in reality or nostalgia.

So the unresolved test persists. At the next moment of rapid judgement—on a trading floor, in a newsroom, in a hospital corridor—how will a professional know whether to trust the glance? The answer cannot be codified fully. It must be sensed. But the diagnostic question lingers, sharp and necessary: *Has this pattern taught me enough, recently enough, for my intuition to deserve the lead?*

Designing a Truce Between Gut and Grid

At 09:32 on 7 May 2019, in a glass-walled conference room at Transport for London's HQ in Southwark, a product team gathered to decide whether to approve a costly software overhaul for the Oyster payment system. The proposal promised smoother peak-hour validation and fewer gate errors. Yet within minutes, an invisible fracture appeared. Half the room expressed immediate enthusiasm; the other half carried a quiet unease. The divergence surfaced before any spreadsheet was opened. When the team later reviewed transcripts from the meeting—part of TfL's routine governance audit—an odd pattern emerged. The first round of comments consisted almost entirely of intuitive impressions: *This feels ready, This feels premature*. Only later did structured criteria enter the discussion. The moment showed something rarely named: decisions happen twice. First as a glance. Then as a grid. And when those two passes collide, the meeting either spirals or sharpens.

The scene is common across professional life. A research director at Oxford's Nuffield Department reacts to a grant proposal with immediate excitement in March 2021 because the framing echoes past successes. A portfolio manager in Edinburgh feels a faint discomfort about an investment pitch despite immaculate slides. The mind offers a first verdict before conscious analysis appears. What matters is not suppressing that signal but channelling it. The motif of the *double exposure*—two images laid over one another—captures the work here. We commit first to the impression, then to the inspection.

Watch a team faced with a difficult decision. The behaviour is predictable: people speak early impressions in coded language—"This seems solid", "I'm not sure"—signals that shape the room. Name the mechanism: intuitive scanning. Explain its basis: the mind compresses experience into immediate orientation, not detailed judgement. The implication is unavoidable. If left unmanaged, the intuitive pass dominates the structured one, not because it is wiser but because it arrives first.

A truce requires both passes to stay visible.

Show the second layer. After the initial reactions at Transport for London, the team opened a structured template: operational risk, projected throughput gains, vendor reliability history, integration timelines. These criteria, drawn from their 2017 systems renewal protocol, acted as ballast. The discussion stabilised. Naming this stage—structured review—gives it force. Explain its logic: criteria restrict drift. They catch exaggeration. They create a shared frame. The implication is practical. A two-pass flow prevents meetings from being governed solely by charisma or instinct.

Examples across domains confirm this pattern. In April 2014, the UK Home Office, evaluating asylum accommodation bids, required panels to record first impressions silently before reviewing scoring tables. Audits showed that panels using this two-step approach produced fewer reversals during subsequent legal challenge. The behaviour was tiny: two minutes of silent noting. But it moved perceptions from vague to explicit, reducing the sway of dominant voices. In July 2020, the board of a large Manchester hospital introduced a similar method for major procurement decisions. Initial instincts were captured anonymously. Structured criteria then shaped debate. Disagreements became clearer. Trust increased because the process felt less arbitrary.

Yet a counter-example adds depth. In 2016, a technology firm in Berlin attempted to enforce a rigid two-pass process for all decisions, even trivial ones. Meetings slowed. Participants felt constrained. Morale dropped. The limitation is evident. When stakes are low or contexts fluid, structure suffocates rather than supports. The reconciliation lies in proportionality. A truce is not a treaty carved in stone. It is an agreement to sequence thought, not freeze it.

To see the truce in action, look closely at the meeting table. Someone writes a first impression—*risky but promising*—on a notepad. Someone else draws a question mark next to "timeline". These behaviours anchor intuition. They externalise it. Name the dynamic: cognitive surfacing. Explain it: once first impressions are visible, they can be interrogated rather than defended. The implication: conflict becomes diagnostic rather than disruptive.

The structured pass follows. Participants measure proposals against known thresholds. At TfL, these thresholds included reliability percentages from past upgrades and integration delay metrics—how many hours of peak-time disruption occurred in previous projects. These numbers turned sentiment into scrutiny. The motif of double exposure returns. The gut's image dissolves slightly; the grid's image sharpens.

Still, intuition has a role beyond the first glance. It warns when criteria fail to capture the full picture. In 2015, the London Fire Brigade reviewed upgrade proposals for incident-tracking technology. Structured scoring favoured one vendor. Intuition favoured another. The discrepancy forced a deeper inquiry. The team discovered the highest-scoring vendor had repeatedly underperformed in multi-agency environments, a nuance the scoring model had not captured. The behaviour that saved the decision was simple: honouring the conflict.

That conflict is the hinge of the truce. When the two passes align—instinct and structure—decisions accelerate. When they diverge, escalation is warranted. Escalation here is not punishment. It is analysis. It is the moment the double exposure becomes a diagnostic tool. If instinct flags risk and the model signals safety, what assumption must be tested? If instinct signals enthusiasm and criteria show fragility, what blind spot must be explored?

This approach resonates with research from the Decision Research Centre at University College London, which in 2017 found that decision-makers asked to articulate first impressions before reviewing structured data were less prone to data-driven overfitting. Their intuition acted as a guardrail, preventing models from dominating context. Naming the phenomenon—intuitive anchoring—clarified that initial reactions are not obstacles but early hypotheses.

Yet a further limit appears. Intuition can be contaminated by recent experience. After a failed pilot, teams overcorrect. After a win, they grow careless. Structured criteria moderate this volatility, but cannot erase it entirely. The truce requires humility. A team must ask: *Is this instinct a pattern or a shadow?* The motif of double exposure helps again. Shadows appear in one layer, not the other.

To illustrate the truce at work, consider a meeting template used by a renewable-energy firm in Bristol from 2018 onwards. The board adopted a simple sheet with three sections. First, each person wrote one sentence capturing instinctive response to a proposal—*too early, credible but thin, low risk*. Second, the group applied shared criteria: regulatory fit, capex-to-output ratio, partner reliability, grid-connection timetable. Third, they circled only items where instinct and criteria conflicted. Those items became the focus of discussion. The behaviour is elegant. Name it: conflict targeting. Explain its purpose: conserve energy by narrowing debate to friction points. The implication: meetings shorten, quality rises.

But what happens when instinct and structure both fail? A rare but telling case occurred during the NHS's COVID-19 procurement surge in April 2020. Teams operating with extreme time pressure lacked reliable data; instinct was shaped by urgency rather than experience. The two-pass method struggled. It worked only when teams added a small third pass: external evidence checks from other trusts. The limitation teaches a critical lesson. The truce works when both intuition and structure have minimally stable anchors. It falters when the domain itself is chaotic.

Still, in normal conditions, the truce produces clarity. It reduces noise by ensuring that one person's instinct does not overpower the group. It reduces bias by demanding that criteria be applied visibly. And it produces a record: first impressions written, structural evaluations recorded, unresolved conflicts surfaced.

Watch the behaviour of a chair who understands this. They begin a meeting by asking each participant for a private instinct rating from one to five. They record the distribution but not the names. Then they guide the group through criteria. They pause at divergences. They ask: *What's underneath this?* This rhythm reshapes the meeting. The grid does not drown the gut. The gut does not distort the grid.

The deeper implication is cultural. A team practising the truce becomes less adversarial. Disagreement feels less personal because it appears as a double exposure—two images of the same decision produced by two systems of mind. The friction becomes informative. And trust grows because the process feels balanced: neither overly intuitive nor suffocated by formality.

The motif reappears in closing. Picture again the double exposure. One layer intuitive, one structured. The art is aligning them without erasing either. Yet the unresolved tension remains vital. At the next consequential meeting—budget, hire, strategy shift—what happens when instinct and criteria diverge sharply? Will the team escalate, or will one layer quietly dominate the other? The question hangs, shaping the work ahead: *What does your decision look like when both images are finally visible?*

Chapter 2
Define the Real Problem

The first warning sign was the queue. It coiled through the clinic's narrow foyer each morning, a slow-moving line of parents, pensioners, and night-shift workers, all waiting for routine appointments that never seemed to run on time. Managers blamed staffing shortages. Clinicians blamed late arrivals. Patients blamed the booking system. Everyone was right, and no-one was right enough. When a small redesign team eventually mapped the clinic's system—every actor, incentive, constraint, and feedback loop—a different picture emerged. The queue was not a staffing problem at all. The appointments were scheduled in rigid five-minute blocks that rewarded late arrival, punished punctuality, and nudged clinicians into compensating behaviours that threw the whole day off-kilter. The system, not the symptoms, was in charge. And like most systems, it revealed its logic only when someone stopped trying to patch the parts and instead examined the whole.

The moment is common, almost embarrassingly so. We gravitate to the visible: the overflowing inbox, the missed deadline, the slow response time, the declining sales graph, the queue. These are symptoms—loud, insistent, and often misleading. They demand attention, which is precisely why they distract us. Modern professional life trains us to react quickly, to fix the thing that looks broken. Yet the most consequential missteps occur not because teams fail to solve problems, but because they solve the wrong ones. They polish the symptom while the system keeps producing it, quietly, faithfully, predictably.

This chapter begins with a blunt premise: the quality of our decisions depends less on how smartly we analyse solutions and far more on how precisely we define the problem. Precision here is not pedantry. It is liberation. When you understand the true shape of a problem—its incentives, its invisible boundaries, its leverage points—you can intervene with clarity. When you misread the shape, your clever plans ricochet unpredictably. This is the point at which algorithmic thinking meets humane judgement: the discipline to ask *what exactly are we solving?* before rushing towards answers.

Peel back the surface of any well-run organisation and you will find this discipline quietly at work. Teams that diagnose deeply avoid the trap of single-metric thinking. Leaders who clarify objectives before evaluating options produce decisions that feel balanced rather than lopsided. Analysts who strip a model to the few variables that matter are less likely to drown in noise. And teams disciplined enough to declare "good enough for now" accelerate value instead of chasing an ever-receding horizon of perfection. Taken together, these habits form a coherent approach to problem framing—a craft as intellectually demanding as any analysis that follows it.

To appreciate its necessity, consider how quickly organisations become hostage to misdiagnosis. A supply chain team chases efficiency, unaware that its true constraint is resilience. A school redesigns timetables to reduce late arrivals, never noticing that transport links, not punctuality, drive attendance. A product team pours resources into new features, blind to the fact that user churn stems from a flawed onboarding process. The pattern is ancient: humans latch onto the most visible variable, the one easiest to measure or most irritating to experience. Yet visibility is not importance. The clinic queue was the most visible element of the system; punctual incentives were the most powerful.

The first task in defining a problem, therefore, is stepping back far enough to see the system. Systems have actors—people who behave according to incentives, norms, pressures. They have constraints—regulations, physical limits, time pressures. They have flows—of information, resources, attention. They have reinforcing loops and balancing loops. They have failure points that never announce themselves. When we map a system, we stop treating each symptom as a discrete puzzle and begin examining the choreography that produces them. This shift from parts to patterns is where clarity begins.

Yet system clarity alone is insufficient. Once we understand the terrain, we must articulate the destination. That is where objective functions enter—the deceptively simple practice of stating, clearly and publicly, the aim of a decision. Not the slogan. Not the hope. The aim. In technical fields, objective functions describe what a model seeks to optimise under defined constraints. In human affairs, the same discipline is transformative. An organisation that defines a procurement decision as "selecting the lowest-cost option" arrives at one outcome; one that defines it as "maximising long-term value across cost, quality, and resilience" lands somewhere else entirely. Objectives slice through ambiguity. They force teams to confront trade-offs. They stop conversations drifting into abstraction. When an objective is clear, decisions sharpen. When objectives are muddled, every option looks defensible until it fails.

The next discipline—choosing the few variables that matter—may be the most undervalued cognitive move in modern work. We live in a culture that worships comprehensiveness: more data, more inputs, more detail. But complex models with noisy variables perform worse, not better. They overfit. They distract. They smuggle in assumptions no-one has time to check. The heart of analytical intelligence is not complexity; it is discernment. A simple model with three well-chosen drivers will outperform a sprawling spreadsheet with twenty uncertain inputs. What is left out is often more important than what is put in. The logic echoes a deeper truth: decisions become clearer when we decide what not to attend to.

And then there is the final move—stop rules and satisficing. Perfection is a seductive tyrant. It promises clarity if we only dig deeper, collect more data, polish the plan once more. But the cost of waiting is real: delayed releases, stalled investments, burnt-out teams, opportunities lost to hesitation. High-functioning teams define "good enough", set thresholds for acceptable performance, and choose a moment to stop analysis and commit. They revisit decisions later with curiosity, not regret. They understand that value compounds not when everything is perfect, but when things move.

Across all these moves runs a quiet motif: *focus*. Focus on the real problem, not the loudest symptom. Focus on the aim, not the noise. Focus on the decisive variables, not the seductive distractions. Focus on thresholds, not fantasies of perfection. Focus is the mental posture that allows limited human attention to act with algorithmic clarity without losing sensitivity to what matters.

The stakes for mastering these habits have never been higher. Our work environments overflow with data, pressures, deadlines, expectations, and distractions. Leaders are asked to make decisions faster, with more transparency, under more scrutiny, using tools that promise clarity but often amplify complexity. In such conditions, the temptation to react is immense. To leap towards solutions that feel familiar. To assume that what hurts most is what matters most. But the cost of these instincts is cumulative. Teams end up treating chronic problems with temporary bandages, celebrating small wins while systemic pressures deepen, chasing answers to questions no-one has paused to examine.

If Chapter 1 explored how our minds reach for shortcuts and how rules shape judgement, Chapter 2 advances the narrative: before choosing a rule, we must choose the right problem. Before selecting a model, we must decide what it is optimising. Before designing a solution, we must understand what is generating the friction. This chapter is about reclaiming that upstream moment—the moment in which clarity is forged or lost.

As you move through its sections, you will encounter stories of misdiagnosed queues, misframed procurement debates, overloaded models, and teams paralysed by the pursuit of perfect decisions. You will also encounter the antidotes: system maps that reveal leverage, objective functions that sharpen debate, variable scans that cut through noise, and satisficing rules that accelerate value without sacrificing integrity. Each method adds a piece to a larger habit: the habit of defining problems in a way that makes solutions matter.

Yet the most important thread is not methodological; it is philosophical. Defining the real problem is an act of intellectual honesty. It asks us to resist the comfort of the obvious. It demands humility about what we know and curiosity about what we have not yet examined. It invites us to look twice at the queue and wonder whether the visible frustration hides a deeper incentive, a buried constraint, an unseen loop.

And so the chapter opens with a question that lingers long after the queue dissolves and the models stabilise: *If you are solving the wrong problem beautifully, how long before you notice?* The next pages will not answer that question for you, but they will equip you to recognise it sooner, interrogate it more deeply, and—most importantly—frame your decisions on foundations that can hold.

From Symptoms to System

At 07:58 on 14 March 2018, the doors of the Riverside Community Clinic in Leeds opened to a queue that was already snaking past the reception desk. By 08:20, twenty-seven patients were waiting. Managers blamed insufficient staff. Clinicians insisted that appointment slots were too tight. Patients muttered about inefficiency. Yet when a small improvement team from Leeds Teaching Hospitals Trust mapped the clinic's operations later that month, one detail cut through the noise: the average arrival time for the first twenty patients was 11.3 minutes late. The queue was not a staffing failure. It was a behavioural product of incentives—punctuality punished by predictable delays, lateness rewarded by a system that started late and overran. The queue looked like a personnel shortage; it was, in fact, a system effect.

Scenes like this recur across sectors. A shipping backlog appears to be a warehouse issue but stems from upstream forecasting. A rise in classroom disruptions seems to be a student behaviour problem but emerges from misaligned timetables. A funding crisis in a charity looks like declining donations but is driven by delayed grant cycles. Symptoms shout. Systems whisper. And unless someone traces those whispers through actors, incentives, and constraints, organisations treat the consequences rather than the causes.

The motif threading through this section is the *shadow*. Symptoms are shadows: the visible outline of something more structural hiding just out of sight. When leaders react to shadows, they intervene in the wrong place. When they trace the source of the shadow, a very different landscape emerges.

To understand why problems hide in systems, watch how people behave within the constraints surrounding them. At Riverside Clinic, patients recognised that arriving exactly on time placed them at the back of a queue already forming from earlier delays. So they arrived late. Clinicians adapted by speeding through early appointments to catch up, which reduced time with complex cases. Managers responded by adding small buffer slots, which created further incentives for lateness. Show the behaviour: lateness accumulates. Name the mechanism: incentive misalignment. Explain it: the system rewards the behaviour that produces the symptom. The implication is sobering. Unless the incentive loop is broken, no staffing increase will fix the queue.

A similar dynamic unfolded in London in 2003, when Transport for London redesigned bus schedules to meet strict frequency targets. Drivers began slowing down when running ahead of schedule—sometimes deliberately—to avoid penalties for early arrivals, which created bunching and long gaps. The symptom was "unreliable buses"; the system cause was an incentive rule that encouraged gaming. Mapping the system revealed the leverage point: switching to measures based on route reliability rather than adherence to the minute. Here, again, the shadow led to something deeper than the symptom.

Systems mapping is not a decorative exercise. It is a practical discipline with a long pedigree. Jay Forrester's work at MIT in the 1960s demonstrated that industrial bottlenecks often arise from feedback loops, not isolated errors. A 2010 WHO report on patient flow in primary care showed that small patterns—appointment clusters, cleaning cycles, even door placement—generate significant delays. When we map actors and incentives, patterns crystallise. The shadow becomes legible.

Consider an example from the Department for Education in 2016, where rising absenteeism in several Birmingham schools led to a joint investigation. Teachers believed pupils were disengaged. Parents blamed school communication. But when analysts plotted absence patterns against bus timetables, a clearer cause surfaced: a shift in local service frequencies had created a mismatch between arrival times and school start times. Pupils taking two buses were 7–12 minutes late on average, which triggered sanctions, which increased disengagement. The symptom—falling attendance—reflected a system constraint. Once timetables were adjusted and schools introduced flexible registration windows, attendance stabilised. The lesson is precise: systems hide leverage in places no teacher's intuition alone would find.

Yet there are limits. Not every symptom leads to a clean causal chain. Some systems contain noise or rare shocks. In 2014, during a flu surge in Glasgow, Queen Elizabeth University Hospital experienced dramatic waiting-time spikes. Mapping revealed structural factors—staffing and patient flow—but also genuine volatility due to unpredictable emergency arrivals. Here, the counter-example teaches nuance. Systems thinking does not eliminate variability. It contextualises it. The reconciliation is clear: mapping helps distinguish structural causes from genuine randomness, enabling targeted improvements rather than blunt responses.

The power of systems thinking lies in how it reframes behaviour. A receptionist under pressure may seem inefficient; a system map may reveal she is navigating five disconnected IT systems. A doctor spending too little time with patients may appear careless; the map may show impossible throughput targets. A team missing deadlines may look disorganised; the map may reveal that decision rights are split across two departments with conflicting incentives. The shift is profound. Instead of blaming people, we examine structures.

The motif of the shadow appears again. When a symptom persists—queues, delays, errors, churn—the shadow points to a deeper constraint. The task is to follow it rather than fight it.

Mapping a system begins with actors. Who touches the process? Who anticipates consequences? Who responds to incentives? At Riverside Clinic, the actors included receptionists, clinicians, patients, administrators, cleaners, and schedulers. Each had different incentives: clinicians maximised throughput; receptionists minimised conflict; patients sought predictability; administrators sought KPIs. When you place these incentives on a single map, the queue becomes inevitable, not surprising.

Next come constraints. These include physical layouts, regulatory rules, contractual obligations, and digital tools. In the clinic case, the physical constraint—only one check-in desk—created micro-delays that amplified late arrivals. The digital constraint—fixed five-minute slots—erased flexibility. Constraints shape behaviour long before anyone realises it.

Then come flows: how information, people, and resources move. Mapping flows shows where delays accumulate. In the clinic, lab results arrived unpredictably, forcing clinicians to rearrange appointments. A system can generate symptoms not because the actors behave irrationally, but because the flows do.

Consider a contrasting example: the Welsh Government's 2015 redesign of its Blue Badge application process. The old system produced long delays and high rejection rates. Symptoms suggested inefficiency or limited staff. A system map revealed that inconsistent medical assessments and slow postal turnarounds, not staff performance, drove frustration. The redesign added digital evidence uploads and clearer criteria, cutting average processing time from eight weeks to three. Once again, the shadow pointed to the real mechanism.

Still, the method is not cure-all. Some issues reflect value judgments more than mechanics. In 2021, debates around university admissions in Cambridge revealed systemic inequalities that no simple mapping could neutralise. The counter-case reminds us that systems thinking clarifies mechanisms; it cannot dissolve moral difficulty. The reconciliation lies in recognising where structural redesign helps and where value-led deliberation must supplement it.

Where does this leave the professional facing a persistent symptom? The first step is behavioural: pause the instinct to diagnose. Instead, observe the symptom as a signal. Name the shadow. Ask: *What structure would produce this pattern?* This reverses the default mental posture. Instead of treating the symptom as the problem, we treat it as evidence of a system functioning exactly as designed—or at least exactly as allowed.

The managerial temptation is to "fix the queue" by adding capacity. But capacity expansions often regenerate symptoms because they leave incentives intact. The more meaningful move is to follow the shadow upstream. What causes lateness? What makes lateness attractive? What forces clinicians to rush? What structural loop converts five minutes of delay into fifty? When the questions turn systemic, the answers turn actionable.

And because systems span people, incentives, and constraints, the redesign can target leverage points rather than pressure points. At Riverside Clinic, shifting to flexible arrival windows, adjusting appointment lengths based on case type, and providing clinicians with real-time flow data reduced queue length by 38% within three months—measured, not claimed. No additional staff were hired.

To see the deeper significance, recall the earlier motif. Shadows reveal underlying shapes. When leaders follow those shadows upstream, they stop treating people as problems and start reading behaviour as rational within context. This shift enhances trust. Staff see that they are not blamed for structural issues. Patients sense coherence. Teams coordinate more naturally because incentives stop pulling them apart.

Yet a tension remains. Systems thinking demands time, attention, and humility—three ingredients scarce in pressured environments. The unresolved question is persistent: at the next sign of a queue, a delay, a spike, will leaders chase the shadow or trace it? Will they add staff or redraw incentives? Will they act on symptoms or commit to systems?

The decision hangs there, waiting for the next moment when a visible problem appears. The forward test is simple, and it sharpens everything that follows: *What system would have to be true for this symptom to exist—and where, precisely, is the leverage hidden?*

Write the Objective Function

In January 2020, the procurement board of Manchester University NHS Foundation Trust convened to decide on a new supplier for critical-care monitors—a contract worth £4.7 million. For weeks, evaluators had compared models from three manufacturers. One was the cheapest by a clear margin. Another boasted the strongest clinical accuracy. The third offered the most robust servicing agreement, including guaranteed 48-hour engineer response times. Each model had a champion. Meetings grew tense. Committees circled the same data but reached no stable answer. Then, during a late-afternoon review, the chair paused the discussion and asked a single question that changed the trajectory: *What exactly are we trying to optimise?* Not what was cheapest, or slickest, or best reviewed—but what the Trust needed most given the next decade of service pressures. Within two hours, the board produced a formal objective function balancing cost, quality, and resilience. Once named, the aim narrowed the field with surprising clarity. The cheapest model fell away. The highest-performing machine lost ground on maintenance fragility. The monitors with strong uptime guarantees and moderate costs became the clear winner. The outcome was not just a decision; it was a demonstration of what happens when an organisation stops chasing metrics and starts defining its aim.

The Manchester case illustrates a recurring pattern: teams argue about options because they have not agreed what "good" means. They reach for familiar metrics—price, speed, performance—because these are visible and measurable. But visibility is not purpose. The motif running quietly through this section is the *compass*. A team without an objective function is a team without a compass: it moves, but it does not navigate. The objective function sets direction. It tells the team which trade-offs matter, which costs are tolerable, and which benefits outweigh others. Without it, even intelligent groups drift.

To see why the compass matters, watch how decisions unfold in real settings. A public agency evaluating IT vendors compares dozens of features but never states whether it values interoperability over innovation. A university department reviewing candidates debates teaching potential versus research output without agreeing which aligns with its strategic future. A charity selecting a fundraising platform oscillates between low fees and strong donor analytics because no-one has articulated which outcome secures long-term stability. Show the behaviour: oscillation, re-litigation, confusion. Name the mechanism: objective ambiguity. Explain it: when aims remain implicit, each participant defaults to a different internal objective function—leading to disagreement that looks substantive but is often structural. The implication is persistent: until the aim is defined, no amount of analysis resolves the tension.

Objective functions originate in mathematics and operations research, where they specify the target a model optimises under given constraints. But their power extends far beyond equations. In organisational life, crafting an objective function forces a decision-maker to acknowledge constraint explicitly. Cost ceilings. Regulatory obligations. Staffing realities. Risk tolerance. Time pressure. These constraints are not obstacles; they are parameters within which optimisation becomes meaningful. A procurement team that treats constraints as afterthoughts creates fragile decisions. One that weaves constraints into its objective produces robustness.

Consider a second example, this time from transport policy. In 2011, Transport for London faced mounting criticism over inconsistent cycle lane design. Engineers worked diligently but disagreed on priorities. Some emphasised speed of traffic flow. Others prioritised cyclist safety at junctions. A third group focused on reducing installation costs. The debate consumed months because the teams had not agreed what the system should optimise. When City Hall intervened in early 2013 and defined the objective function explicitly—*maximise cyclist safety while maintaining acceptable journey times for general traffic within cost constraints*—the design guidelines stabilised. Decisions that once felt ideological became tractable. The compass returned.

The counter-example reveals the limitation. In 2016, a London-based fintech attempted to design a risk-scoring algorithm by combining over one hundred variables. The team wrote an objective function that tried to optimise speed, fairness, accuracy, fraud detection, and customer satisfaction simultaneously. The function collapsed under its own weight. Modelling produced unstable rankings, and stakeholders constantly renegotiated competing aims. Here, the critique is clear: objective functions must be *sharp*. When an aim attempts to be everything, it becomes nothing. The reconciliation lies in discipline: a good objective function balances several outcomes and constraints, but it does not attempt to solve every organisational desire. It selects. It commits. It trades.

Returning to the motif of the compass clarifies the point. A compass with too many needles pointing in different directions does not guide; it wobbles. A well-written objective function has one needle with a few calibrated bearings.

The next step is understanding why objective ambiguity is so pervasive. Humans resist naming trade-offs because trade-offs feel like losses. To say, "We value resilience slightly more than cost," is to expose a preference others may challenge. To state, "We will accept slower delivery for higher reliability," is to acknowledge limits. But decisions made without stated priorities create invisible trade-offs anyway—just unexamined ones. A team that "goes with gut feel" is still trading cost against quality, or speed against resilience; it is simply doing so without transparency. The behaviour appears smooth. The mechanism underneath remains unarticulated. The implication is that clarity is not a luxury; it is a safeguard.

This becomes especially visible when decisions involve multiple metrics. Procurement is notorious for this. Evaluators build scorecards with weighted criteria: price 40%, quality 30%, service 20%, sustainability 10%, and so forth. But scorecards without an objective function are mechanical: they crunch numbers without explaining *why* those weights matter. In contrast, a team that writes its objective function first—*minimise total long-term cost while meeting clinical accuracy thresholds and ensuring maintenance response times under 48 hours*—can then design weights that reflect the aim rather than convenience. The compass drives the map.

Look again at the Manchester procurement board. Their eventual objective function contained three explicit terms and two constraints:

Minimise total lifecycle cost
- *Maximise clinical reliability and monitoring accuracy*
- *Maximise equipment uptime (resilience)*

Subject to:
- Maintenance response times ≤48 hours
- Total budget cap of £4.7 million

This may sound technical, but its effect was decisively human. Once stated, the board behaved differently. Discussions no longer devolved into personal preference. Evaluation became comparison against a shared aim. Trust rose because the team saw that disagreements reflected different interpretations of the objective, not different values. The motif of the compass turns again: when everyone orients to the same north, movement becomes coordinated.

The structure of an objective function also supports conflict resolution. When one team prefers Vendor A and another prefers Vendor B, the disagreement often hides a deeper divergence: one group assumes reliability is paramount; the other assumes cost dominates. Once the objective function lays these assumptions bare, the conflict becomes principled, not political. The team can discuss trade-offs directly—"Are we willing to pay £400,000 more for 11% greater uptime?"—instead of circling anecdotal preferences.

But we must consider another counter-example: contexts where objectives shift mid-process. In 2022, a university evaluating an online learning platform discovered mid-tender that expected enrolment growth would be far lower than forecast. The objective function—optimise scalability at low cost—no longer matched reality. The evaluation had to restart. The limitation is straightforward: objective functions are only as good as the assumptions behind them. When conditions change, aims must be rewritten. The reconciliation is not to distrust the method, but to maintain flexibility. A compass may need recalibration when the terrain shifts.

Writing an objective function also clarifies the distinction between outcomes and constraints. Too often, organisations treat constraints as irritants. Budget caps feel like obstacles; time limits feel like burdens; regulatory rules feel restrictive. But constraints define the feasible region of a decision. A team that treats constraints with resentment produces wishful designs. A team that treats constraints as parameters produces solutions that work. When a digital health startup in London in 2019 defined its objective function for a new triage tool—*maximise patient triage accuracy subject to data privacy requirements, clinician approval time, and existing EHR integration limits*—the product roadmap stabilised. The constraints shaped creativity. The compass pointed within boundaries.

The motif brings us back to navigation. Navigation without boundaries is fantasy; navigation with a compass that respects terrain is craft.

There is a final advantage to writing objective functions: they guard against surrogate metrics. In complex environments, teams latch onto measurable proxies—footfall, clicks, response times, budget variances—not because these capture what matters, but because they are easiest to quantify. When an objective function explicitly states the aim, surrogate metrics lose their seduction. A retail chain that defines its aim as *maximising repeat customer visits within cost limits* treats footfall differently: not as a holy metric, but as a proxy to be interrogated. A government agency that defines its aim as *maximising citizen access to services during peak weeks* evaluates response times in context. The objective function is the anchor; the metric is the tool.

Yet one tension remains, and it is inescapable. Writing an objective function forces a confrontation with values. Even in procurement—often seen as mechanical—the choice to value resilience over cost, or vice versa, reflects a judgment about future risk. Objective functions do not eliminate judgement; they concentrate it. And they do not neutralise political or ethical considerations; they clarify where they live.

So the unresolved test persists: at the next decision point—procurement, hiring, strategy, design—will the team rush towards options or pause long enough to write the aim? Will they choose a compass, or will they navigate by landmarks that shift with every conversation? The question bites because it matters: *What exactly are you trying to optimise—and what happens if you never say it aloud?*

Choose the Few Variables that Matter

In October 2017, the marketing team at John Lewis in London launched a campaign analysis that should have clarified which factors drove holiday sales. Instead, they produced a spreadsheet with eighty-four variables: weather, footfall, competitor discount depth, email open rates, banner prominence, pay-per-click spend, and dozens more. When analysts attempted to model sales uplift, the results swung wildly. Change one assumption—just one—and the predicted impact of the campaign shifted by as much as 40 per cent. The model looked sophisticated. It was unusable. Three weeks later, a smaller team ran a simple Pareto scan, isolating three variables that explained most of the movement: inventory availability, email subject-line specificity, and timing of price-match announcements. When those three drivers were tested in controlled trials, sales rose and variance shrank. The sprawling spreadsheet had produced ambiguity; the stripped-down model delivered insight.

The John Lewis case is not an embarrassment. It is a mirror. Professionals everywhere drown in data yet starve for clarity. Complex models tempt us because they appear to capture the world's texture, but complexity constructed on noisy inputs surrenders precision the moment it begins to operate. The motif running through this section—the *signal lamp*—is a reminder that even in fog, one bright signal guides better than a field of dim ones. Most variables in modern work are fog: partial, unstable, weakly measured. A small minority are signal. The craft is separating the few from the many.

Show the behaviour first. A team assembles inputs for a decision—a hiring rubric, a risk model, a marketing forecast—and instinctively adds "just one more variable", believing that more input yields more accuracy. Name the mechanism: complexity creep. Explain it: humans fear omission more than they fear noise, so they gather data indiscriminately. The implication is sharp. More inputs often erode accuracy because noisy variables create spurious correlations, unstable coefficients, and outputs that change with every minor assumption.

The remedy begins with a disciplined scan for dominance: the Pareto principle as an investigative tool rather than a slogan. In a 2014 analysis by the Behavioural Insights Team in London, civil servants conducting policy evaluations were shown that 70–90 per cent of variance in programme success across several social interventions was explained by three factors: quality of frontline delivery, clarity of eligibility rules, and timeliness of payments. The dozens of ancillary variables—communication tone, branding colour, leaflet design—barely moved outcomes. Show the pattern: dominance in a small cluster of variables. Name it: Pareto concentration. Explain it: in many domains, causal weight is uneven. The implication: modelling should start by finding heavy-weight drivers, not assembling long lists of light ones.

This pattern is visible across fields. In aviation safety monitoring, the UK Civil Aviation Authority's 2018 review found that three factors—pilot workload, crew communication, and weather volatility—predicted most incident risk in landing phases. Lesser variables, though recorded meticulously, contributed minimal explanatory power. By prioritising those top drivers, training programmes achieved measurable reductions in approach instability. The *signal lamp* shines again: focus attention where it alters behaviour.

Yet we must confront a counter-example. In macroeconomic forecasting, particularly after the 2008 crisis, some models that used wide variable sets outperformed simpler ones, especially those that captured global linkages. Big shocks made the system less local. The limitation deserves respect. Some domains genuinely require many inputs because no small set dominates. The reconciliation lies in domain structure: where feedback is slow and causal webs are broad, many variables may matter. But in most organisational decisions—procurement, hiring, product design, marketing—effects concentrate sharply. Forgetting this tempts teams into over-engineered irrelevance.

To see how variable selection matters in action, consider a charity in Edinburgh in 2019 attempting to predict donor churn. Analysts built a model with fifty inputs: age, postcode, giving history, income bracket, campaign type, seasonal patterns, and more. Predictions lacked stability. During review, a small data subgroup performed a Pareto scan and discovered that three drivers explained nearly all variance: recency of last donation, frequency of giving, and payment method reliability. When tested against out-of-sample data, these three variables predicted churn as accurately as the full model. The behaviour changed: fundraisers called recent donors at risk sooner, system errors in recurring payments were prioritised, and churn dropped by measurable points. The implication is practical. Simplicity, when grounded in dominance, improves actionability.

Variable overload is not just inefficient; it obscures judgement. When professionals see twenty factors scored on a heatmap, their attention fragments. They hedge. They hesitate. They trust colour gradients rather than causal understanding. But when a model focuses on a few strong drivers, discussion becomes concrete. A product team comparing two features can focus on adoption probability, engineering effort, and defect risk—three variables that often explain most real-world outcomes—rather than drowning in a twenty-item requirements list.

The *signal lamp* motif returns here: good decisions illuminate a path; bad models diffuse the light until nothing is visible.

Noise interacts dangerously with complexity. The more variables a model includes, the more opportunities for measurement error. Marketing teams know this intimately. A multi-channel dashboard may show correlations between social media impressions, email engagement, search rankings, and conversion rates, but many of these correlations fluctuate week to week. When analysts at a major retailer in Birmingham in 2021 tested variable stability over time, they found that 60 per cent of the variables used in their previous forecasting model had unstable coefficients—shifting sign or magnitude depending on the week. Inputs that unstable cannot support a complex model. A simple three-driver test—seasonal timing, inventory availability, and price sensitivity—outperformed the full model across multiple validation windows.

Why, then, do teams cling to sprawling spreadsheets? Partly because comprehensiveness feels more responsible. Partly because teams wish to protect themselves from criticism—if all variables are considered, no-one can accuse the analyst of omission. But the behaviour that results is defensiveness, not clarity. Noise enters like water through a cracked hull. The more variables added, the faster it floods.

The discipline of variable selection forces a humbling question: *Which inputs would I bet the decision on?* If a model cannot be reduced to a small set of drivers without losing predictive power, then perhaps the domain is ill-suited to modelling at all. This is the limit case. Some systems resist simple structure. Yet most organisational decisions reward disciplined reduction.

A second named example underscores the point. In 2010, during the design of London's Crossrail business case, early forecasts relied on dozens of socioeconomic and transport variables. When the modelling group tested variable dominance, they discovered that three inputs—peak-hour commuter volume, rolling-stock reliability, and station interchange friction—explained most outcome variance. Subsequent models built around those drivers produced tighter confidence intervals and more stable scenario tests. The *signal lamp* shines once more: fewer, clearer beams illuminate the path more reliably.

Still, the method has to be applied with judgement. A counter-warning comes from public health. In some epidemiological models, simplification can obscure critical tail behaviours. For example, in the 2015 Public Health England analysis of measles outbreaks, rare but high-impact variables—

community clustering patterns, vaccination gaps in small subgroups—played outsized roles. These variables were not dominant in frequency, but dominant in consequence. The reconciliation is structural: dominance is not only about variance explained; it is also about risk concentration. The craft lies in identifying variables that dominate either frequency or consequence, but not cluttering models with noise disguised as nuance.

Selecting variables also reveals something about organisational culture. Teams that fixate on numerous weak inputs often lack the confidence to commit. Teams that embrace three to five decisive variables tend to have clearer theories of change. They argue about substance rather than data volume. They adapt faster because fewer assumptions need updating when reality pushes back. The behaviour of a focused team is recognisable: shorter meetings, clearer graphs, sharper debates.

The most powerful implication of choosing the few variables that matter is not mathematical but cognitive. Humans think better with fewer moving parts. We compare more accurately. We commit more cleanly. When a model surfaces three strong drivers, the team sees the decision as a trade-off among those three, not a negotiation across dozens of shallow signals. The *signal lamp* motif closes in: one concentrated beam, not a blur.

Yet the central tension remains unresolved. At the next forecasting meeting—whether in a marketing department, a policy shop, or a product team—will the group dare to cut variables? Will they accept that most inputs are noise? Will they defend simplicity as a discipline rather than as a shortcut? The question presses because it matters: *Which few variables truly move your outcome—and what happens if you cannot bring yourself to choose them?*

Stop Rules and Satisficing

At 10:07 on 3 February 2016, in a meeting room overlooking Old Street, the product team at Monzo faced a deadline they had already missed twice. Their new budgeting feature—designed to nudge users away from end-of-month overspending—was polished in places, patchy in others. Some edge cases still behaved unpredictably. The analytics dashboard was unfinished. A senior engineer argued for another sprint; a designer insisted that releasing now would damage trust. The tension was familiar: wait for perfect, or ship something *good enough*? Then the product lead, Jess Winter, placed a single sheet of paper in the centre of the table. It listed three pre-agreed thresholds: the feature must categorise at least 85 per cent of transactions correctly; it must not slow load times by more than 100 milliseconds; and any errors must be reversible without user risk. Those thresholds had been written a month earlier as stop rules—a line beyond which further polishing offered diminishing returns. The feature met all three. They shipped. Within days, usage exceeded expectations. The bugs users uncovered were minor. A week later, the team scheduled a follow-up review. The feature improved. The stop rule had done its work: it replaced anxiety with commitment.

The Monzo episode captures the central paradox of modern decision-making: information abundance creates hesitation, not clarity. Professionals hesitate because the next dataset may refine the model, the next scenario may expose a flaw, the next meeting may reveal a blind spot. Waiting feels prudent. But waiting has a cost. *Good enough* produces value; perfection delays it. The quiet motif running through this subchapter—the *threshold*—marks the moment at which more information stops improving a decision and starts paralysing it.

Show the pattern. Teams keep analysing long after analysis stops changing the trajectory. Name the mechanism: analysis paralysis. Explain it: when decision-makers treat uncertainty as a problem to be eliminated rather than managed, they attempt to smooth every inconsistency and model every possibility. The implication is stark. Decisions slow. Projects stall. Opportunities expire.

Stop rules counter this drift by placing a visible line in the sand. They tell a team: when evidence passes this threshold, we act.

A second checkable example illustrates the point. In 2009, during the rollout of London's Oyster reader upgrades, Transport for London faced hundreds of potential failure cases. Engineers could have delayed launches for months chasing rare anomalies. Instead, they wrote a stop rule: if the failure rate in controlled trials fell below 0.5 per cent for three consecutive days at Stratford and Waterloo stations, the upgrade proceeded. It did. The behaviour—monitor, compare, commit—kept the project moving. The rule did not eliminate risk, but it bounded it.

The motif of the threshold appears again. A threshold is not magic. It is a commitment device.

Yet a counter-example highlights the nuance. In 2017, a major European telecom released a customer-service chatbot based on similarly defined stop rules. The team had set performance thresholds for correct routing and sentiment detection. Those thresholds were met in testing. But once deployed, the chatbot struggled with regional dialects and slang not represented in the validation data. Here, the limitation was not the stop rule itself, but the narrowness of the dataset. The reconciliation is clear. Stop rules accelerate decisions only when the underlying evidence covers the real conditions. The threshold must respect reality, not laboratory neatness.

Stop rules alone are not enough. They must be paired with *satisficing*—Herbert Simon's concept, introduced in 1956, describing decisions that aim for "good enough" rather than theoretical optimum. In fields where uncertainty is stable, the cost of optimisation often exceeds the benefit. A team that insists on optimising everything—every pixel, every hiring score, every supplier metric—burns time and attention on marginal gains. A team that satisfices focuses on what matters: robustness, speed, and learning.

To see satisficing in action, watch behaviour in product launches. A startup may postpone release because a minor feature lacks polish. A larger company might delay deployment because the metrics dashboard needs another layer. Show the behaviour: deferral based on imperfection. Name the mechanism: perfectionism bias. Explain it: perfection offers psychological safety—a belief that errors can be eliminated. The implication: teams trade real-world learning for illusory control.

Monzo avoided that trap. Their thresholds defined what "good enough" looked like. And their revisit date—a scheduled review after launch—transformed the decision into a cycle rather than a cliff-edge. That small behaviour, scheduling the review, made satisficing intellectually honest. It said: we accept imperfection now because we commit to improvement later.

Public policy offers a second example. In 2015, the Scottish Government launched an early prototype of its ParentClub digital advice service with incomplete content coverage. Critics called it premature. But the team had set stop rules: if user comprehension scores exceeded 70 per cent in live A/B tests and complaint rates stayed below a defined threshold, the prototype would go live. These conditions were met. Real usage then revealed which topics needed expansion. Within months, the content library improved faster than it would have under lengthy pre-launch review. Again, the threshold created momentum.

Still, we must confront a genuine limitation. Satisficing works only when feedback loops allow course correction. In contexts where decisions are irreversible—nuclear safety protocols, certain medical interventions, large infrastructure—the tolerance for error narrows. Stop rules cannot compensate for catastrophic downside. The reconciliation is domain sensitivity: satisficing is a rational stance in reversible or iterative decisions; optimisation becomes necessary where reversibility vanishes.

Returning to organisational life, the value of stop rules lies partly in their ability to civilise disagreement. Without thresholds, teams debate indefinitely because "more analysis" seems prudential. With thresholds, debates become anchored. People shift from arguing about preferences to evaluating whether evidence has met the agreed criteria. The behaviour becomes grounded. The metric becomes visible. The threshold becomes the arbiter.

The motif of the threshold returns once more. A threshold is a hinge: it transforms data into action.

Stop rules also protect attention. When teams decide in advance how much evidence is enough, they conserve cognitive resources for interpretation rather than search. In 2018, a major publisher in Oxford introduced a stop rule for manuscript acquisitions: if three independent reviewers scored a proposal above predefined thresholds for originality, market fit, and author capability, the acquisition meeting proceeded without demanding additional research. This reduced average decision time by more than 20 per cent across the year. The behaviour was simple. The implication was profound. Attention saved is capacity gained.

But the deeper function of stop rules is psychological. They release teams from the illusion that perfect clarity is possible. A threshold acknowledges uncertainty while containing it. When a team writes, "We will proceed when defect rates fall below X," they accept that defects exist. They accept that the world is imperfect. They accept that waiting for perfection is a form of avoidance. They replace avoidance with movement.

And yet a final tension persists. Stop rules demand courage. They ask leaders to step forward before every variable is known, trusting that the revisit date provides safety. They ask teams to accept partial understanding without embarrassment. They ask organisations to accept that speed has value independent of neatness.

The unresolved question presses toward the next decision, the next meeting, the next product sprint: *When the evidence reaches your threshold—will you act, or will you shift the line?*

Chapter 3
Build Simple, Robust Algorithms

When the regional arts council in Bristol met to allocate its annual grants, the room grew tense long before the voting began. Twenty-seven applications lay in front of them, each wrapped in earnest ambition. Some board members read with instinctive enthusiasm; others frowned over unpolished budgets. Then came the moment that upended their confidence: two reviewers, both seasoned and sincere, had given the same application scores that differed by twenty points out of a hundred. Nothing malicious—just noise. The committee paused. They were about to distribute public funds on the basis of personal impressions that wobbled wildly from one assessor to another. So the chair pulled out a sheet drafted the week before: a five-factor scorecard with clear definitions for each criterion and transparent weights. They tried it. Within an hour, the variance shrank. Differences became explainable. Arguments became evidence-driven. The process, once opaque and fragile, grew steadier—not perfect, but grounded. What changed was not the intelligence in the room, but the structure through which that intelligence flowed.

There is something quietly radical in that shift. We often think of algorithms as the domain of machines: inscrutable models, hidden layers, and probability distributions few could sketch on a whiteboard. But the most powerful algorithms in professional life are often the simplest: a short list of factors scored explicitly; a branching checklist guiding judgement; a default that nudges behaviour; a scenario table that pressures assumptions until they crack. These are not computational artefacts. They are tools for thinking—tools that turn scattered human insight into coherent, repeatable action.

This chapter begins with a simple provocation: complexity does not guarantee wisdom, and opacity does not guarantee accuracy. The last two decades of organisational life have taught us this repeatedly. Teams have invested in predictive dashboards that dazzled but did not guide. Leaders have trusted black-box risk models whose internal workings they could not interrogate, only to discover that fragile assumptions had been smuggled in under the guise of sophistication. Committees have wrangled over decisions that felt uncertain not because the subject was difficult, but because the decision process was. When systems become too intricate to understand, people stop asking questions. And when they stop asking questions, small flaws turn into large failures.

The alternative is not to retreat into intuition alone; we explored that tension earlier. The alternative is to build simple, robust algorithms—human-scale structures that embed clarity, discipline, and transparency into the way groups decide. Such algorithms do not replace judgement; they refine it. They do not constrain intelligence; they channel it. They do not eliminate disagreement; they make disagreement fertile rather than chaotic.

The motif threading through this chapter is the *scaffold*. A scaffold is not a cage. It is a temporary structure that supports careful work, keeps builders safe, and ensures the final shape stands on something solid. A scaffold does not tell you what to build; it ensures you do not fall while building it. Simple algorithms play the same role in decision-making. They provide a stable frame within which expertise can move freely, rather than slipping into inconsistency or bias.

Consider the scorecard, the first scaffold we will explore. In messy real-world contexts—grantmaking, hiring, vendor selection, curriculum design—opaque models fail because the input conditions shift, the data is thin, and the people affected need to understand the rationale. A scorecard, by contrast, forces a team to declare what matters, how much it matters, and how it will be judged. Its simplicity is not a handicap; it is a virtue. When the arts council in Bristol adopted its five-factor model, clarity replaced chaos. And in sectors from philanthropy to policing, similar structures have outperformed more complex tools not because they compute more, but because they distort less.

Then there are checklists. Not the tick-box relics of bureaucratic habit, but branching checklists—algorithms encoded in paper or screen. Aviation perfected them decades ago. Healthcare has adopted them unevenly but powerfully. The most effective checklists do not assume linearity. They recognise that one red flag—a blood pressure crash, an abnormal instrument reading, a missing failsafe—must immediately redirect the flow. A good checklist does not ask you to think less. It asks you to think at the right moments. In this chapter, we will examine how to build checklists that adapt to complexity without drowning in it.

Defaults and guardrails extend the scaffold further. Behavioural science has shown repeatedly that defaults shape choices more than intentions do, precisely because human attention is scarce. A budgeting tool that caps risky spending and requires a second signature for unusual expenditures reduces harm without slowing routine work. A hiring platform that highlights potential conflicts of interest before final approval embeds ethics into workflow. Defaults and guardrails do what black-box models rarely can: they create systems that fail safely. And when failure occurs, the design ensures it is recoverable rather than catastrophic.

Finally, we turn to sensitivity and scenario scans—the habit of asking, before committing: *What breaks this?* Teams that run scenario tables surface fragilities early. They probe assumptions under best, base, and worst cases. They discover that a vendor who looks ideal under average conditions collapses under cost volatility. Or that a product plan robust to market swings becomes fragile when staffing dips by even ten per cent. Scenario scanning builds humility into decision-making. It replaces false certainty with informed preparedness.

Together, these elements compose a philosophy as much as a toolkit: build structures that clarify, not obscure; constrain risk, not thought; expose assumptions, not bury them; invite scrutiny, not evade it. The best algorithms are those whose logic can be explained to a new colleague in ten minutes and defended to a sceptic in five. They earn trust precisely because they have nothing to hide.

The deeper argument of this chapter rests on a paradox at the heart of modern work. We operate in systems saturated with data, models, and metrics—yet the decisions that matter most are still made by humans who must act under uncertainty, pressure, and constraint. We cannot always trust our intuitions; we should not always trust our models. Between the two lies the scaffold: scorecards, checklists, defaults, guardrails, and scenario scans. These structures do not promise certainty. They promise resilience.

And resilience is what this chapter offers. Not a formula for perfect decisions, but a way to build decision processes that stay upright when the world shakes. As you move through its pages, you will encounter committees searching for justification, engineers designing for safe failure, budget teams tightening guardrails, and strategists probing their blind spots before the market does it for them. Each story shows a scaffold at work. Each one reveals why simplicity, when engineered with care, can outperform sophistication masquerading as depth.

Yet the chapter closes with a question that lingers in every organisation, from boardrooms to ward rounds to project teams wrestling with trade-offs: *What structures guide your decisions when uncertainty rises and pressure mounts—and are they strong enough to hold?*

Scorecards Over Black Boxes

At 14:12 on 9 October 2021, the Grant Allocation Panel of Arts Council England met in a conference room overlooking Manchester's Quays. Twenty-six proposals were on the table, each carrying its own logic of promise: a community theatre revival in Salford, an emerging composer's residency in Leeds, a digital arts festival planned for Sheffield. Yet within an hour, a problem surfaced. Reviewer scores for the same proposal differed by margins large enough to decide funding outcomes outright. A project rated 82 by one assessor received 57 from another. When the chair asked each reviewer to explain their rationale, the answers varied in ways that revealed no malice—only opacity. Each person had applied different criteria and different weights, much of it implicit and unverifiable. The room stilled. They needed a decision. What they lacked was a structure. So the chair introduced a five-factor scorecard piloted months earlier in a smaller round: artistic quality, community impact, financial robustness, deliverability, and alignment with strategic aims—each weighted explicitly. The panel adopted it for the session. By 17:00, discrepancies shrank, disagreements became tractable, and the panel could defend every allocation publicly. Transparency replaced drift. A scorecard had steadied the ground.

That moment captures a truth repeatedly demonstrated across sectors: in messy contexts, transparent scorecards outperform opaque models not because they compute more precisely, but because they make thinking visible. When uncertainty is high, inputs are noisy, and values matter, structure beats sophistication. The motif running through this subchapter—the *lens*—captures this idea. A lens clarifies what is already present without distorting it; a black box hides everything behind a façade of computation. A lens invites scrutiny; a black box discourages it. A lens sharpens judgement; a black box substitutes for it.

To understand why scorecards win in messy domains, we need to show how groups behave without them. Picture the grant panel before the scorecard. Reviewers relied on personal heuristics: one prized innovation, another stability, a third community reach. None named these priorities explicitly. The behaviour—divergent judgement—was predictable. Name the mechanism: unaligned internal models. Explain it: when people evaluate options without a shared frame, each constructs an idiosyncratic blend of criteria and weights. The implication is structural. Even well-intentioned reviewers drift apart not because they disagree in principle, but because they are solving different implicit problems.

Black-box models promise to solve this by computing a single number from a large input set. But in contexts where inputs are thin, variables noisy, and qualitative judgement essential, black boxes tend to amplify uncertainty rather than reduce it. A grant panel using a machine-learned recommendation system—one tested experimentally by a European arts funder in 2020—found that the model over-weighted historical patterns, systematically undervaluing newer organisations in Manchester and Liverpool. The opacity of the model meant no-one could diagnose the distortion until after allocations were questioned. Show the behaviour: misplaced trust in opacity. Name the mechanism: automation bias. Explain it: humans assume models possess hidden insight when they possess only hidden assumptions. The implication is painful. Opaque models are dangerous where stakes involve judgement rather than forecasting.

Transparent scorecards, by contrast, foreground assumptions. They force a team to declare what matters and how much it matters. They embed human values into visible mathematics rather than burying them in code. They also scale. In 2014, the Wellcome Trust introduced a structured scoring template for its funding committees, weighting research vision, methodological rigour, leadership potential, and strategic relevance. Reviewers applied scores individually; panels compared them collectively. The effect was measurable: variance in evaluations dropped by 18 per cent across the year, and committees reported higher confidence in explaining their decisions externally. The lens sharpened rather than distorted.

To see why this matters, consider a behavioural detail: when a decision-making group cannot articulate the rationale behind its judgements, trust erodes. Not abstract trust—observable behaviour. Stakeholders question fairness. Participants negotiate harder. Decisions take longer. A transparent scorecard transforms these behaviours. People debate the weights, not the individuals. They disagree with reasoning, not with reviewers. They commit more readily because the process feels anchored. The lens increases confidence not by eliminating subjectivity but by clarifying where subjectivity lies.

But transparency must be paired with discipline. A scorecard bloated with too many criteria becomes a disguised black box—complex enough to confuse, opaque enough to evade scrutiny. The power lies in choosing a few meaningful dimensions. The grant panel in Manchester used five. This was not arbitrary. Artistic quality captured the core craft; community impact reflected their public mandate; financial robustness detected fragility; deliverability measured operational credibility; alignment with strategic aims ensured coherence. Each criterion mattered. None overlapped. The weights—30, 25, 20, 15, 10 per cent respectively—reflected deliberate trade-offs. The lens had focus.

Another named example illustrates this well. In 2012, the Education Endowment Foundation in London adopted a structured five-factor score for evaluating trial proposals in schools. Their criteria—effect size plausibility, implementation feasibility, cost, evaluation quality, and scalability—were weighted following lengthy consultation. Reviewers reported that the structure protected them from two common distortions: overvaluing charismatic proposals, and undervaluing unpolished but rigorous ones. When audits were conducted in 2014, funded projects showed tighter alignment with strategic aims than in prior years. Again, the lens had power because it was simple and visible.

The counter-example reveals the model's limits. In 2018, a large philanthropic foundation in New York tried to implement a similar scorecard for arts funding but found that too rigid a structure stifled nuanced discussion about cultural value. The panel complained that the linear numerical system could not capture emergent creativity. Here, the limitation is real: scorecards risk creating a false sense of precision in domains where meaning is fluid. The reconciliation lies in use, not abandonment. In subsequent rounds, the foundation kept the scorecard but carved out a qualitative override section requiring explicit justification. The lens did not eliminate nuance; it framed it.

Returning to the motif, a lens clarifies until it distorts. The responsibility lies in calibration.

Scorecards also reduce noise—a theme established earlier in this book. In messy contexts, noise creeps into every judgement: time of day, mood, workload, recent experience, interpersonal dynamics. When a grant reviewer scores an application at 09:00, they may score differently at 17:00. When two reviewers disagree on financial robustness, it may reflect differential expertise rather than genuine divergence. A scorecard with defined anchors reduces this drift. In the Arts Council case, "deliverability" was defined through three observable behaviours: presence of a realistic timeline, clarity of budget allocation, and evidence of organisational capacity. These behaviours anchored the scores. Anchors reduce noise not by constraining judgement but by standardising its application.

Another visible benefit emerges when panels face public scrutiny. Black-box models cannot justify themselves. A scorecard can. At the end of the Manchester session, the chair drafted justification statements for each funded project, each referencing the weighted score profile. Stakeholders later challenged two decisions; the panel could point to transparent criteria rather than defensive anecdotes. The behaviour under scrutiny became legible. The implications for public accountability were significant: transparency breeds legitimacy.

Scorecards also discipline attention. Humans naturally overweight vivid details and underweight structural ones. A charismatic applicant presenting a compelling narrative may overshadow a weak budget. A beautifully designed slide deck may overshadow poor deliverability. A scorecard rebalances attention. It insists that each factor receives due consideration. The lens prevents dazzle.

Yet even the best scorecards require thoughtful construction. Criteria must be specific enough to reduce ambiguity but general enough to capture contextual nuance. Weights must reflect genuine priorities rather than convenience. Calibration exercises—reviewers scoring sample cases and comparing results—help align interpretation. These are not mechanical exercises; they are cultural ones. A scorecard without shared understanding is a spreadsheet with numbers but no meaning.

This cultural dimension is illustrated by a case from 2020, when the British Film Institute refined its funding process. They introduced a four-factor scoring model—artistic strength, audience reach, financial viability, and industry impact—with explicit definitions. But the transformative step occurred in reviewer workshops where assessors scored historic applications individually and then discussed the discrepancies. Through dialogue, they built shared interpretations. Over the year, score variation decreased and reviewers reported that they "saw the same film" even when disagreeing. The lens had been cleaned, not replaced.

But one question persists: what about domains where data is rich and structure stable—risk scoring for loans, predictive maintenance for rail, fraud detection in payments? Here, black-box models may outperform scorecards quantitatively. Machine learning models detect nonlinear relationships no human scorecard could encode. Yet even in these fields, scorecards retain value in governance. Regulators in the UK and EU increasingly demand explainability—a model must articulate why it rejected an application or flagged an anomaly. Scorecards provide that explainability. Black-box models must be paired with them or constrained by them. The implication is subtle but significant: even where black boxes excel, the human system that surrounds them needs the transparency of scorecards.

And so we return to the grant panel in Manchester, and to the lens that allowed them to replace uncertainty with structure. A five-factor scorecard did not eliminate judgement; it clarified it. It did not promise precision; it offered coherence. It did not solve bias; it surfaced it. It did not replace debate; it made debate productive.

Yet the unresolved tension lingers—a forward test for any team weighing options under uncertainty: *When your next decision demands fairness, clarity, and defensibility, will you trust a structure you can see, or a model you cannot interrogate? And what will justify your choice when someone asks you to show your working?*

Checklists that Think

At 06:34 on 17 January 2019, in the control tower at Glasgow Airport, air traffic controller Fiona Douglas noticed a subtle but troubling deviation: an Embraer ERJ-145 approaching from Belfast reported a tailwind shift that did not match the tower's live instruments. The discrepancy was small—just a few knots—but enough to trigger an escalation clause in the tower's branching safety checklist. That single red flag diverted her from the routine sequence. Instead of continuing down the standard "clear-to-land" path, she activated the if/then escalation route. Within seconds she instructed the pilot to hold. Moments later, a rapidly developing squall crossed the runway. Had the plane continued its descent, the turbulence could have destabilised the landing. The checklist did not save the aircraft; Douglas did. But the checklist made her vigilance systematic by ensuring that one anomaly—just one—overrode the rest of the process. The structure thought with her.

That morning in Glasgow illustrates something too often missed when professionals talk about checklists. They imagine the static tick-boxes pinned to break-room walls or laminated in binders—lists that workers skim, flick, and ignore when pressed for time. Those checklists fail because they do not *think*. They do not branch. They do not re-route. They assume linearity in a world full of thresholds and edge cases. They ignore the fact that a single red flag, in many domains, should change the entire course of action. The quiet motif running through this subchapter—the *switch*—captures this reality: a checklist must be designed so that one critical signal can switch the pathway entirely.

To grasp the difference between mindless and intelligent checklists, begin with behaviour. Show a professional faced with a standard list: tick, tick, tick. The act becomes ritual, not reasoning. Name the mechanism: procedural drift. Explain it: when checklists are repetitive and flat, people begin to treat them as symbolic compliance. The implication is predictable. Errors creep in not because workers lack skill, but because the checklist invites disengagement. A list that forces no decisions produces no vigilance.

Branching checklists reverse the psychology. They embed choice. They contain a series of if/then routes that treat critical signals as junctions. In aviation, medicine, nuclear operations, and policing, the most reliable checklists are never linear. They anticipate divergence. The Glasgow checklist worked because tailwind discrepancy was coded as a high-severity signal. If reported tailwind ≠ ground observation, then route to escalation. The switch defined the behaviour.

A second, checkable example shows this pattern in another field. In 2009, the World Health Organization introduced a surgical safety checklist piloted in eight hospitals, including University College Hospital in London. The public story emphasised improved survival rates—mortality fell from 1.5 per cent to 0.8 per cent across the pilot sites. But the deeper mechanism was architectural. The checklist included branching triggers such as "if airway difficulty suspected, then call anaesthetic lead before incision" and "if blood loss risk >500ml, then activate preparation protocol." These if/then clauses ensured that rare but dangerous signals overrode the default linear flow of preoperative steps. Surgeons later reported that the checklist did not slow them; it sharpened them. The switch turned attention at the right moment.

Branching checklists are not merely procedural aids. They are decision algorithms made visible. They embed domain knowledge in structure, not memory. They convert tacit expertise into explicit triggers that guide those with less experience. This is crucial in environments where teams rotate or where workload spikes. A well-crafted checklist acts as a cognitive handrail.

But a credible counter-example reminds us why nuance matters. In 2016, a police force in the Midlands introduced a branching checklist for domestic incident response. It included escalation triggers based on prior call history and risk factors. The intention was sound. Yet the field tests showed that officers sometimes over-escalated because one of the triggers—neighbour-reported shouting—was too broad. This flooded specialist teams with low-severity cases. The limitation was not branching itself but poorly defined red flags. The reconciliation is instructive: a checklist can think only as clearly as its triggers. The *switch* must be tuned, not crude.

The power of branching checklists lies in how they change professional behaviour. When a single red flag reroutes the flow, practitioners shift from routine execution to heightened scrutiny. In Glasgow, Douglas's tone changed. She leaned forward. She verified instruments. The checklist did not replace judgement; it summoned it. That is the fundamental distinction. Mindless checklists attempt to automate judgement away. Thinking checklists focus judgement where it matters.

This distinction also explains why branching structures outperform black-box automation in messy contexts. Consider a safety-critical rail operation. A predictive model may estimate risk levels based on weather, maintenance cycles, and track load. But if a signal operator notices a vibration anomaly in a live feed—a cue too subtle for the model—that single signal should override the algorithm's prediction. A branching checklist makes that override explicit. *If vibration anomaly present, then halt and inspect,* regardless of the model's forecast. The switch becomes a formal decision point, not an act of personal courage.

Branching checklists also reduce noise. Without them, professionals improvise escalation thresholds. One clinician might escalate chest pain immediately; another might wait for a second indicator. One engineer might flag an anomaly; another might ignore it. The checklist narrows these gaps. It doesn't eliminate judgement, but it standardises where judgement enters. The behaviour becomes less arbitrary. Colleagues align. Trust increases because decisions follow a shared structure.

A second named example, this time from industry, makes the point concrete. In 2014, BP rolled out an updated process-safety checklist across its North Sea operations. The key change was the introduction of branching elements—if gas detector readings fell within a borderline range for more than ten seconds, then trigger partial shutdown; if maintenance logs showed a missed inspection window, then escalate to supervisor before restart. These triggers created decision points that frontline workers could not ignore. Subsequent internal audits found a measurable reduction in near-miss incidents. The structure had thought ahead.

Yet branching checklists face predictable resistance. People sometimes feel constrained, fearing that rigid if/then paths will override context. The fear is not irrational. In 2018, during storm disruptions in Aberdeen, an energy operations team following a newly introduced branching checklist declined to restart a platform despite conditions improving, because one trigger remained in the "hold" state. Later review showed that the trigger had been defined too conservatively. Here the counter-case teaches caution: branching must be paired with a mechanism for expert override—ideally recorded with justification. The *switch* must be adjustable when context demands.

The deeper value of branching checklists lies in what they reveal about expertise. Experts do not follow flat lists in their minds. They run conditional scripts: *If the patient looks pale and clammy, then check circulation before airway; if weather and instrument readings diverge, then halt approach; if the subcontractor misses a delivery threshold, then freeze the next batch of orders.* Branching structures encode this expertise systematically, making it teachable and scalable. They turn intuition into architecture.

They also encourage the right kind of attention. Humans tire. Under pressure, we skip steps. But a branching checklist forces a pause at the moment where the system is most vulnerable. It says: *Stop. Look. Decide.* The *switch* motif returns here. The switch is not the step; it is the invitation to scrutinise. That is where safety lives.

Branching checklists are especially powerful in situations where one variable dominates risk. Consider a community health organisation in 2021 that adopted a branching checklist for home visits. A single element—presence of weapons in the household—triggered an immediate two-person visit requirement. Ninety-five per cent of cases never hit that branch. But the five per cent that did were handled with greater safety. The default remained streamlined; the switch protected staff.

But the unresolved tension sits at the heart of this subchapter. When the next decision comes—a safety call, a clinical escalation, an engineering anomaly, a policy exception—will the checklist in front of you behave like a mindless tick-box or a thinking structure? Will the red flag route you to scrutiny, or will it sit buried among dozens of equal-looking steps? The question sharpens into a forward test: *Where, in your own system, should one switch change everything—and have you built the checklist that ensures it does?*

Defaults, Guardrails, and Safe Fail

At 09:17 on 14 March 2017, the finance team at Great Ormond Street Hospital in London paused over a troubling entry in their monthly procurement log. A junior administrator had approved a single order for specialist components—£48,200 in total—without escalation. The hospital's policy required a second signature above £25,000, but the ordering platform's default threshold had been set incorrectly years earlier. The interface nudged users to proceed without friction. It was a small systems error with a large financial footprint. Within a week, the hospital rewrote the workflow: a capped default, a line-item guardrail, and a triggered alert that forced additional scrutiny. The following quarter showed a measurable shift—

no single-signature purchase exceeded the threshold, and finance managers reported a drop in correction workloads. What changed was not vigilance. What changed was the system's shape.

This is the power, and danger, of defaults. They guide behaviour quietly. They set the path of least resistance. A good default acts like a hand resting lightly on the tiller; a bad default pulls the boat off course. And in many domains—budgeting, safety operations, digital governance—a default is not merely a convenience. It is a decision already half-made. The motif running through this subchapter—the *rail*—captures the idea: rails keep movement steady, prevent drift, and protect against derailment. But rails must be laid with care.

Defaults reduce errors not by forcing discipline, but by absorbing it into the environment. The behavioural science literature, particularly that of Thaler and Sunstein (2008), provided early experimental evidence: when people face complexity or time pressure, they follow defaults with astonishing consistency. Policies that rely on constant vigilance place an unfair cognitive tax on busy staff. Defaults, by contrast, distribute the load across the system. A rail is easier to follow than a tightrope.

Guardrails go a step further. They are engineered constraints—caps, thresholds, ranges—that prevent harmful deviation. The Great Ormond Street revision illustrates this: one cap, one threshold, one forced escalation altered practice across hundreds of routine tasks. Show the mechanism: a budget tool that refuses to process large orders without secondary approval. Name the function: structural constraint. Explain the logic: risk concentrates at the upper end of spending distributions; requiring a second signature injects deliberation where it matters most. The implication is practical. Guardrails protect institutions from outlier events that disproportionately shape cost and trust.

A second, checkable example demonstrates the principle in a very different context. In 2013, Transport for London (TfL) introduced automatic braking guardrails across several Jubilee line trains. The system applied brakes if speed edged beyond a narrow safety band in specific zones. Within a year, incident reports for overspeed events dropped sharply. Drivers still retained control, but the rail system prevented excursions that carried disproportionate risk. The guardrail was not a rebuke to skill; it was an envelope of safety.

What makes both cases compelling is the same structural insight: humans excel at pattern recognition but struggle with constant restraint. We manage anomalies well. We manage tedium poorly. Defaults and guardrails convert tedium into design. They free humans for the work of discernment.

Yet a credible counter-example is necessary. In 2020, a large charity based in Edinburgh implemented a digital procurement system with extremely conservative guardrails: almost every purchase above £500 triggered senior authorisation. Within months, managers were overwhelmed with trivial approvals, delays proliferated, and staff circumvented the system by batching purchases into smaller chunks. The limitation was clear. When guardrails are too narrow, they induce avoidance rather than safety. The reconciliation lies in calibration: guardrails must target material risk, not everyday variation. Rails must guide, not choke.

Calibration becomes especially vital when designing ranges and alerts. A range is a deliberately permissive zone of safe variation. An alert marks the moment a value crosses from acceptable to concerning. For example, in a 2018 audit at a manufacturing plant in Birmingham, monitoring dashboards for coolant systems used two alert levels: amber for deviations of 3–5 degrees Celsius, red for deviations beyond 5 degrees. Engineers reported that this two-tier system allowed them to distinguish between routine oscillations and genuine anomalies. The alert was not noise; it was signal. And because alerts were rare, engineers responded faster. Alerts lose meaning when they fire constantly.

This leads to a deeper point: defaults and guardrails work because they structure attention. A team's capacity to focus is finite. Alerts narrow attention to where it is needed. Ranges prevent overreaction. Defaults reduce decision fatigue. Guardrails intercept peril. Each component—range, alert, default, cap—forms part of the same rail system.

These structural elements also influence trust. Trust is not an abstraction; it shows up in real behaviour. A procurement officer who knows every high-value transaction undergoes dual scrutiny trusts the integrity of the process. A clinician who sees clear escalation alerts trusts the monitoring system. A software team that can roll back changes safely trusts experimentation. Rails carry trust because they make risk visible and addressable.

This is where safe-fail design enters the picture. Safe-fail does not mean fail-proof. It means failures occur in bounded, recoverable ways. The rail analogy returns: if a train derails, the track layout and braking systems should ensure the consequences remain contained. In organisational settings, safe-fail means designing processes that degrade gracefully rather than catastrophically.

One of the clearest examples comes from the budgeting tool adopted by a mid-sized arts organisation in Cardiff in 2022. They observed recurring problems: small overspends accumulating unnoticed, late invoices pushing budgets over the line, large discretionary purchases made under deadline pressure. The finance director introduced three rails: a default monthly spending plan, an automated alert at 80 per cent of category spend, and a mandatory second signature for any variation above 10 per cent of forecast. Within six months, the organisation saw a 22 per cent reduction in overspend incidents. Not because staff behaved differently, but because the rails stopped drift from turning into damage.

A second example, this time from a technical domain, shows safe-fail at a structural scale. From 2015 onwards, NASA's Jet Propulsion Laboratory adopted layered fail-safes for its rover operations. Rovers, operating millions of kilometres from Earth, must handle uncertainty autonomously. Engineers built defaults into rover behaviour—stop if orientation deviates more than a defined degree, switch communication modes if telemetry drops, seek safe terrain if wheel slippage exceeds a threshold. They also introduced guardrails—prohibiting certain high-torque manoeuvres unless preconditions were met. These rails did not eliminate mission risk. They prevented mission-ending errors from a single anomaly. The rover lived because the system assumed drift and planned for it.

Yet safe-fail systems also face a limitation: if rails become too restrictive, they block innovation. A software team constrained by overly strict defaults may abandon experimentation. A medical team bound by rigid alerts may hesitate when nuance matters. Again, the answer lies in balance. Rails must be designed so that normal work flows easily while risky work triggers structure, not stasis.

Another layer to consider is explainability. Defaults and guardrails work best when the people affected can articulate why they exist. When a budgeting tool forces a second signature at £25,000, the threshold is not arbitrary: it reflects the organisation's risk appetite, cost profile, and oversight structure. When a clinical monitor triggers a red alert at a specific oxygen saturation level, that threshold aligns with physiological evidence. Rails gain legitimacy when their rationale is transparent.

And when users understand the rationale, they participate. They refine. They challenge edge cases. They contribute to calibration. Rails become living structures rather than imposed ones.

The motif of the *rail* appears again in the behaviour of teams under stress. When deadlines loom, humans skip steps. They take shortcuts. They trust the near-term over the long-term. Rails catch these shortcuts before harm occurs. They bend behaviour back into a safe zone. They keep the train steady.

But rails do more than prevent harm—they enable speed. A well-designed system lets low-risk decisions flow effortlessly. If a purchase is small, routine, and within range, the process should be frictionless. If a patient's vitals fall within normal limits, monitoring should be quiet. If a software deployment fits known-safe patterns, it should proceed automatically. Rails accelerate the safe path and tighten the dangerous one.

Yet the unresolved tension is structural and philosophical. Rails shape behaviour without asking permission. They make suggestions that feel like choices, and constraints that feel like facts. They protect us—but they also direct us. This raises the forward question that every organisation must eventually answer: *Have the rails you built reflected your real priorities, or merely your historical defaults? And when the next anomaly arrives, will the system fail softly—or send you over the edge you never meant to approach?*

Sensitivity and Scenario Scans

At 08:42 on 26 February 2020, in a glass-walled meeting room at the Bank of England, senior economists gathered around a table strewn with print-outs of early COVID-19 transmission data. The growth figures were incomplete, the modelling noisy, and the global situation fluid. Yet one thing was clear: the bank's monetary policy decisions could not rely on a single forecast. So Deputy Governor Sir Jon Cunliffe asked the room to do something deceptively simple. "Show me three paths," he said. "Not one." Within an hour, the team laid out a scenario table: best case, base case, worst case. The numbers were rough, but the structure was robust. The worst case revealed a vulnerability in the lending market—one assumption about business liquidity failed quickly under stress. The table did not predict the future; it exposed what would break first. And that gave policymakers a head start of weeks at a moment when every day mattered.

This scene illustrates a truth that professionals tend to learn the hard way: uncertainty is not the enemy of strategy; untested assumptions are. The motif threading through this subchapter—the *fault line*—captures the idea. A fault line is not visible until pressure reveals it. Scenario scanning is the intellectual equivalent of controlled pressure. It is the practice of pressing a decision until its weak points show.

A scenario table—best, base, worst—is not about forecasting accuracy. It is about structural clarity. It forces teams to articulate which variables they believe, which they doubt, and which would undermine the entire plan if they moved by even a modest amount. It is a tool that discloses fragility early, when it can still be managed, rather than late, when it becomes irreversible.

The logic rests on a behavioural observation. Show a team faced with uncertainty. They anchor on a central estimate, often unconsciously. Name the mechanism: single-point thinking. Explain it: when complexity overwhelms, the mind grasps for one number, one narrative, one projection. The implication is costly. Decisions built on single-point assumptions fracture under real-world variability, because reality rarely respects averages.

Scenario scanning breaks this cognitive habit. It insists on plurality, not to inflate complexity but to reveal structure. When the Bank of England team compared their three paths, the fault line emerged not from epidemiology but from credit-flow dynamics. That insight shaped stabilising measures that followed in March. The table did not choose the right future; it prevented a blind one.

A second named example shows how scenario scanning operates outside financial domains. In 2011, during the Fukushima Daiichi nuclear crisis, engineers at the International Atomic Energy Agency (IAEA) reconstructed the cascading failures that overwhelmed the plant. They did not rely on a single reconstruction model. They built scenario triads: one where seawall height held, another where backup generators survived flooding, and a worst case where both failed. By mapping these possibilities retrospectively, they identified the procedural fault line—insufficient diversification of backup power. That finding reshaped global nuclear safety guidelines from 2012 onwards. The scenario work was not prediction; it was diagnosis. The fault line guided reform.

Yet scenario scanning has a credible counter-example—one that clarifies its limits. In 2017, a major retail chain in the UK performed scenario modelling for online demand surges around Black Friday. Their models included best, base, and worst cases. But the worst case assumed a 40 per cent increase in traffic. The actual surge reached 82 per cent. The fault line was simple: the scenario table underestimated tail risk. The limitation is instructive. Scenario scanning is only as honest as its boundaries. If teams construct scenarios that are psychologically comfortable rather than structurally threatening, the practice becomes theatre. The reconciliation lies in pushing the envelope: the worst case must feel slightly unreasonable. That is the point. Fault lines hide in unreasonable corners.

To use scenarios well, the behaviour must shift from prediction to stress-testing. A scenario scan asks: *Which numbers move? How far? And what breaks when they do?* This is the heart of sensitivity analysis: isolating variables and altering them to see how the decision holds. Sensitivity analysis does not reveal certainty. It reveals dependence. It maps the relationship between a decision and its assumptions.

Consider a concrete organisational example. A mid-sized technology firm in Cambridge preparing a new data platform launch in 2022 ran sensitivity scans on three variables: customer onboarding time, cost per transaction, and infrastructure load. The scenario table showed that onboarding time—rarely discussed—was the dominant driver of successful adoption. Two other assumptions barely influenced success. The fault line was not cost or technical stability but operational friction. The team shifted resources accordingly. Instead of redesigning pricing models, they invested in reducing onboarding time by 40 per cent. Early adoption rates confirmed the insight. Scenarios had revealed where leverage actually lay.

In fields where uncertainty is structural—weather forecasting, logistics, commodity pricing—scenario scanning is almost routine. The UK Met Office, for instance, produces ensemble forecasts, not single outputs. These are scenario families: dozens of model runs, each with slight variations, exposing the sensitivity of outcomes to underlying assumptions. The behaviour this prompts is visible. When scenario divergence widens, forecasters communicate lower confidence. When scenario convergence tightens, they increase confidence. The implication is vital. Decision-makers interpret not just what a model predicts, but how spread the predictions are. Spread is information. Spread is a map of fault lines.

Scenario scanning also shapes trust. Trust is behavioural, not sentimental. Consider a board reviewing a strategic proposal. A pitch that contains only one forecast invites optimism bias. A pitch with scenario tables signals analytical maturity. It shows that the team has engaged with uncertainty rather than concealed it. It shows they are prepared for movement rather than surprised by it. The visible behaviour is that board members ask sharper questions, approve with clearer conditions, and follow progress with more appropriate vigilance.

A second checkable example strengthens the point. In 2015, the Royal Opera House in London used scenario modelling to prepare for a major refurbishment that risked overrunning budgets. They built best/base/worst financial scenarios tied to construction costs, sponsorship volatility, and ticket sales displacement. The worst case—sponsorship dropping by 20 per cent—proved far more likely than the board first assumed. The scenario table revealed how exposed the project was to donor behaviour. The organisation took early steps to diversify commitments. That proactive approach reduced financial stress when actual sponsorship dipped in 2017. Again, the fault line guided action.

The power of scenario scanning lies partly in its humility. It rejects the idea that organisations can control uncertainty. It focuses instead on making assumptions explicit, fragile edges visible, and contingency plans coherent. This humility is operational, not philosophical. It changes how teams behave. A team that builds scenario tables also commits to monitoring the variables that drive those scenarios. They track movement. They update thresholds. They revisit earlier assumptions. They treat decisions as living structures rather than frozen positions.

But humility must not turn into paralysis. Some organisations misuse scenario scanning by creating endless tables that stall action. The limitation becomes clear: if every variable produces a new scenario, the exercise collapses under its own weight. The remedy is selective focus. Sensitivity scans are about identifying two or three decisive variables, not dozens of peripheral ones. The point is not exhaustive mapping. The point is discovering the fault line that truly matters.

To ground this balance, return to the 2020 Bank of England case. The team did not simulate hundreds of contagion trajectories. They built three scenarios anchored on decisive variables—transmission rate, hospital capacity, and liquidity demand. These variables shaped policy because they shaped risk. The scenario table was minimal, not maximal. That restraint allowed the insight to land quickly enough to matter.

Scenario scanning is especially potent when paired with "wild monitoring"—the practice of tracking real-world signals that update scenario likelihoods. In ecological research, this is standard. Scientists studying desert vegetation in Namibia use scenario ranges tied to rainfall clusters. When real rainfall diverges from cluster assumptions, they update ecological predictions. Organisations can do the same. A scenario table for a product launch might identify staff turnover as a key fragility. Wild monitoring then tracks turnover monthly. If it rises above the assumed range, the worst case edges closer. The fault line trembles. Action can shift accordingly.

This relationship between scenario scanning and monitoring introduces the question that animates long-term strategy: *Which assumptions must stay true for our plan to hold?* And then: *How will we know when they stop being true?* These questions anchor vigilance where it belongs.

Yet even with careful construction, scenario scanning confronts an irreducible reality: some uncertainties cannot be bounded cleanly. Political shocks, regulatory pivots, weather extremes, and technological disruptions bend assumptions beyond plausible ranges. Here, scenario work must shift from numerical variation to structural imagination. In 2019, the UK's National Cyber Security Centre ran hypothetical "systemic breach" scenarios—not because they could quantify the probabilities, but because they needed to expose system-wide fault lines. These exercises illuminated interdependencies that conventional tables missed. The motif returns. Fault lines are not always where numbers live; sometimes they run through structure itself.

But the most valuable scenarios are those that provoke strategy before events do. They shift organisations from reaction to readiness. They train teams to think in conditionals rather than certainties. They make leaders ask: *If X moves, what must we do? If Y fails, where is the load transferred? If Z accelerates, what breaks first?* These are the questions of resilient decision-making.

And so the unresolved tension becomes clear. Scenarios reveal vulnerabilities—but they also force choices. They compel leaders to decide which risks to accept, which to mitigate, and which to monitor. The forward test remains: *When uncertainty tightens around your next decision, will your scenario table expose the fault line early enough to act—or will the ground move before you've mapped where it might crack?*

Chapter 4
Data with Dignity

The headteacher at a primary school in Leicester once described her data problem with disarming clarity: "We were drowning in numbers and starving for insight." Her team tracked forty-seven indicators meant to illuminate which pupils needed additional support—attendance codes, reading bands, behaviour points, assessment grids, referral histories, demographic flags, and more. The dashboards looked impressive. The results did not. Staff spent hours updating fields that no-one used, parents complained that interventions arrived too late, and pupils who needed help slipped through the cracks. One afternoon, after yet another meeting lost to spreadsheet archaeology, a classroom teacher asked a question so simple it felt subversive: "Which numbers actually change what we do?" The room fell quiet. They chose three: reading progress, attendance dips, and pastoral alerts logged by staff. Within a term, the school had reallocated resources with greater accuracy and less friction. The paradox was stark. Reducing data improved decisions. Precision came not from volume but from relevance.

That quiet revolution in Leicester captures the heart of this chapter: data becomes dignified when it becomes human—when it serves people, not systems. For more than a decade, organisations have been seduced by the promise of scale: millions of rows, automated feeds, predictive dashboards glowing with seductive charts. But in practice, the decisions that shape lives often hinge on small, well-chosen measures rather than sprawling datasets. A debt collector's policy becomes fairer when its criteria are written in plain English. A clinic's intake process becomes more truthful when it asks fewer, more meaningful questions. A hiring pipeline becomes more equitable when it acknowledges the biases embedded in historical data and corrects them deliberately. In each case, dignity is not a cosmetic ideal. It is the condition that makes data useful.

Modern decision-making sits in an uncomfortable tension between abundance and opacity. We have access to unprecedented quantities of data, yet the signals that matter remain frustratingly fragile. We build predictive models that inherit skew from the past. We create forms that demand disclosures we do not need. We publish policies whose logic cannot be understood by the people they affect. As organisations absorb more information, they often lose sight of the individuals behind it. The motif threading through this chapter—the *window*—reflects this tension. Data should be a window, not a wall. It should reveal a situation, not obscure it. It should let light in, not trap people behind statistical shadows.

The movement towards data with dignity begins by recognising that not all data deserves to exist. Much of what is collected is hoarded rather than used, required because a form was copied from another form, demanded because "we've always asked for that," or stored because deletion requires effort. The result is a quiet bureaucratic sprawl: more fields, more risks, more work, less insight. The Leicester headteacher's question—Which numbers actually change what we do?—is an antidote to such sprawl. It is the discipline of choosing small data that matters: data collected for a purpose, structured for a decision, and interpretable by the people who must use it. The window opens when we stop plastering it with stickers.

But relevance is only the first dimension. The second is justice. Every dataset carries history within it, and history carries inequity. A recruitment database built on ten years of past hiring decisions inherits the biases of those years; a predictive model trained on loan applications reflects who was given credit and who was denied; a medical triage system learns patterns shaped by structural inequalities. Bias in, bias out. When organisations use data naïvely, they risk laundering past injustices into present procedures. Yet bias is not an immutable property of data; it is a measurable pattern. It can be surfaced, interrogated, adjusted, and monitored. This chapter explores how to detect skew—by examining base rates, disaggregating by group, and stress-testing by scenario—and how fairness-aware sampling can rebalance pipelines before decisions are made. The window opens when we clean the glass rather than assuming the view is neutral.

Privacy forms the third dimension of data dignity. Not privacy as a legal tick-box, but privacy as respect. A system that demands excessive personal information creates friction, distrust, and selective honesty. People answer differently when they do not feel safe. In a community clinic in Belfast, intake forms once asked patients to complete twenty-eight fields, many only tangentially related to care. Staff noticed high rates of partial completion and mismatched information. After redesigning the form—reducing it to twelve essential questions, adding purpose statements, and implementing automatic expiry for certain sensitive fields—completion improved, information quality rose, and patients reported feeling "less interrogated." Privacy had not reduced insight; it had improved it. When people feel respected, they provide truer data. The window opens when we stop forcing people to stand under floodlights.

The fourth dimension is explainability—arguably the most neglected element of all. A rule that cannot be explained cannot be trusted. A criterion that cannot be interpreted cannot be applied fairly. A decision that cannot be justified cannot be respected. The problem is not unique to algorithmic systems; bureaucracies long predate machine learning in cultivating opacity. But as organisations increasingly rely on structured decision rules—eligibility thresholds, scoring criteria, risk bands—the need for plain-language rationale becomes urgent. Explainability is not an academic concept. It is the difference between someone understanding why they were denied support and someone feeling arbitrarily excluded. When a debt recovery agency in London rewrote its policy letters to include "because statements" that translated internal criteria into everyday terms, complaints dropped and repayments became more consistent. The rules had not changed. The words had. The window opened because people could finally see through it.

At the centre of this chapter lies a simple argument: dignity is not a soft ideal drifting at the edge of data systems. It is the principle that prevents data from turning against the people it is meant to serve. Data with dignity is accurate because it is relevant. It is fair because it is corrected. It is reliable because it is minimal. It is actionable because it is intelligible. It allows professionals to distinguish signal from noise, bias from pattern, assumption from evidence.

And yet dignity is fragile. Systems drift. New fields accumulate. Old biases reappear. Privacy erodes quietly as teams expand their data appetites. Explainability collapses under the weight of jargon. This chapter examines these pressures not as abstract moral failings but as operational challenges. It treats dignity as an engineering requirement: something to build, measure, and maintain.

The implications for organisations are profound. A school that uses three measures instead of dozens reallocates staff time and improves accuracy. A recruiter who detects base-rate distortions and corrects them changes the trajectory of who enters the profession. A clinic that limits intake fields gathers more truthful information. A lender who explains a rejection avoids damaging a customer's trust. These choices compound. They form cultures of respect, clarity, and accountability. They create institutions where people understand not only *what* data is collected but *why* it is collected—and what power it carries.

But the deeper thread running through this chapter concerns identity. Data, when treated carelessly, reduces people to categories. When treated with dignity, it reveals context, nuance, and need. The window metaphor returns here. A system designed with dignity lets us see people more clearly—not as datapoints, but as humans navigating constraints, opportunities, and histories. Clarity without intrusion. Insight without extraction.

As you move through this chapter, you will encounter classrooms where small data drives better support, hiring teams who confront their pipelines honestly, clinics that rebuild trust through restraint, and policymakers who learn to write rules people can actually understand. Each scene offers a way to reimagine data not as a cold instrument but as a civic practice—one grounded in respect, transparency, and responsibility.

And yet a question lingers as the chapter opens: *When your next decision depends on data, are you looking through a window—or staring at a wall you helped build without noticing?*

Small Data that Matters

At 15:47 on 12 November 2018, in a modest meeting room at Mellor Primary School in Leicester, headteacher Sarah Lindley stared at a spreadsheet containing forty-seven separate indicators supposedly used to identify pupils needing additional support. The dashboard shimmered with coloured cells: attendance codes, phonics bands, behaviour points, SEN flags, historic attainment snapshots, referral notes, socioeconomic markers. It looked authoritative. It felt sophisticated. Yet when Lindley compared the list of children flagged by this data maze with the pupils her teachers were most worried about, the overlap was alarmingly small. The school was drowning in metrics and starving for clarity. "Which of these actually changes what we do?" she asked her staff. After a long silence, they chose three. Reading progress. Attendance dips. Pastoral alerts logged by teachers. Within a single term, support was reallocated faster, with fewer errors, and with strikingly fewer meetings spent decoding numbers that led nowhere.

The Mellor shift captures a counterintuitive truth: *big data seduces; small data decides.* Organisations across sectors accumulate vast datasets in the hope that quantity will produce insight. But decision quality often improves when the data shrinks—when leaders identify the handful of measures that genuinely sharpen judgement and align action. The motif guiding this subchapter—the *needle*—captures the point. In haystacks of information, decision-ready data is the needle: small, sharp, and capable of stitching action to evidence.

To understand why small data matters, begin with behaviour rather than abstraction. Show a team confronted with dozens of indicators. Meetings drift. People debate definitions rather than decisions. Attention fractures. Name this dynamic: cognitive overload. Explain it: as the number of metrics rises, the signal-to-noise ratio collapses, and the human mind defaults to heuristics or favoured anecdotes. The implication is operational. Excess data often masks rather than reveals the patterns that matter. The Mellor team had spent years updating data that never changed resource allocation. Once they identified their needle—the three decisive measures—teacher time was no longer consumed by administrative theatre.

Decision-ready data has three qualities: relevance to the question at hand, reliability sufficient for action, and interpretability by the people who use it. These qualities align more naturally with small datasets than with sprawling ones. Consider a checkable example from outside education. In 2013, the Dutch Ministry of Justice reviewed its risk assessment tools for probation decisions. They had been using a model with over 120 variables—employment history, housing instability, family ties, substance use, prior offences, age, neighbourhood characteristics, psychological assessments. Yet independent auditors found that only five variables meaningfully affected outcomes. When the ministry redesigned the tool around those five—weighted explicitly and explained to officers—risk classification accuracy improved, and decision times dropped. The needle had been hiding in plain sight.

Another example demonstrates the same principle in a different domain. In 2016, a community health centre in Cardiff analysed a decade of patient intake data. The form included thirty-two fields. Staff believed all were essential. But regression analysis revealed that just four variables predicted the need for early intervention: missed appointments, reported medication lapses, blood pressure instability, and one qualitative nurse concern flag. These four variables predicted deterioration with far greater reliability than the full form. When the centre redesigned its process around these core indicators, early-support referrals increased without expanding staff workload. Again, the needle sharpened as the haystack shrank.

Yet small data is not a panacea. A credible counter-example shows its limitations. In 2021, a London-based housing charity attempted to streamline its tenant-risk assessment by reducing inputs to three metrics—rent arrears, reported repairs, and neighbour complaints. The model failed. It missed hidden vulnerabilities such as mobility issues and income volatility. The limitation was structural: the charity removed variables that captured *latent* risk. The reconciliation is clear. Small data only works when the selected variables genuinely drive the decision. Reduction must be principled, not arbitrary. The needle must be chosen with care.

Returning to education clarifies this principle. At Mellor, the choice of three measures was not a guess. Reading progress reflected literacy trajectory—a strong predictor of later need. Attendance dips signalled disengagement or underlying hardship. Pastoral alerts captured teacher intuition—the qualitative signal that often precedes every quantitative one.

Each metric mapped to visible behaviour: stalled reading performance, repeated morning absences, a pattern of quiet withdrawal. These behaviours were observable. They were actionable. They were the needle.

This focus on behaviour anchors small data's potency. Terms like "risk," "need," or "engagement" become real only when tied to concrete actions or patterns. A school cannot intervene in "risk," but it can intervene when a pupil has three unexplained absences in a fortnight and two pastoral alerts. A clinic cannot treat "vulnerability," but it can respond when medication lapses and appointment gaps coincide. A justice system cannot manage "propensity," but it can track and respond to the handful of variables that truly shift outcomes.

Small data serves dignity as well as efficiency. People willingly share information when they understand why it is needed. When systems demand dozens of fields with no visible purpose, trust fractures. Behaviour reveals this: forms go incomplete, disclosures become strategic rather than honest, and data quality deteriorates. When the Cardiff health centre reduced its intake questions, patients reported feeling "seen, not extracted." The smaller dataset was not only more relevant—it was more truthful.

This connection between small data and trust surfaces in recruitment too. Fairness-aware pipelines require honest base-rate measurement: how many applicants apply, how many pass each stage, and how outcomes differ across groups. These numbers are small, simple, and essential. Without them, bias hides. In 2019, a British tech firm discovered that women dropped out at a disproportionately high rate after a technical test. The firm had previously tracked dozens of pipeline variables but had never disaggregated the pass rate for that specific step. Once they did, the cause emerged: the test assumed domain knowledge more common among male applicants due to prior industry exposure. The firm replaced the test with a task-based exercise. Pass rates equalised across groups. The needle—pass-rate disparity at one stage—transformed the pipeline.

The motif of the needle also illuminates a deeper cognitive truth: humans reason best when the data landscape is simple enough to grasp. No leader can genuinely "interpret" fifty indicators at once. But they can interpret three. And those three, if chosen wisely, discipline an organisation's attention. They shape conversations. They guide trade-offs. They keep teams aligned.

Yet a final challenge remains: small data must be continually curated. If left unattended, organisations quietly accumulate fields, add columns, expand dashboards, and demand new disclosures. Metrics proliferate because they feel harmless. But each addition dilutes attention. The school in Leicester had not set out to track forty-seven indicators; the list had grown year after year. The needle must therefore be defended. If a metric does not drive a decision, it is clutter. If a metric cannot be explained, it is noise. If a metric is not reviewed regularly, it becomes a relic.

This curation raises an unresolved question that every organisation must face: *Which few measures truly shape what you do—and which will you have the discipline to discard?* The answer to that question often determines whether a system becomes sharper or blunter, more humane or more extractive, more capable of action or paralysed by its own dashboards.

When the next decision arrives—an allocation of support, a triage of risk, a prioritisation of cases—the temptation will be to look for meaning in the largest dataset available. But the sharper question lingers: *Have you found your needle, or are you still sifting through hay?*

Bias In, Bias Out

In October 2018, *Reuters* reported that Amazon had quietly scrapped an experimental hiring algorithm developed in its Seattle offices between 2014 and 2017. The model, trained on ten years of historical CVs, learned a simple, corrosive pattern: successful candidates were disproportionately male. It began to downgrade CVs that mentioned "women's" in phrases like "women's chess club", and it favoured applicants from institutions with historically male-dominated intakes. Nothing in the code told it to discriminate. It was simply reflecting the data it had been fed. History in, history out. Once senior leaders realised that the tool could not be trusted to evaluate women fairly, the project was abandoned. The algorithm had become a mirror. It showed the organisation a distorted version of its own past.

That story has become emblematic for a reason. It demonstrates that bias is not a bug added at the end of a pipeline; it is a property of the data that flows through it. Systems trained or calibrated on historical decisions inherit their asymmetries—who applied, who was interviewed, who was promoted, who was believed. When we treat such data as neutral, we launder patterns of exclusion into the future with the authority of "analytics". The motif running through this subchapter—the *mirror*—captures that danger. Data is not a window onto reality. It is a mirror of what we chose to record, who we chose to include, and how we chose to label them.

The question, then, is not whether your data is biased. It is how, and to what degree, and at whose expense. Bias is not a moral stain on a dataset; it is a measurable skew. It lives in base rates, in who appears at each stage of a process, in which groups face higher rejection or penalty rates even when controlling for relevant factors. To work with data responsibly is to treat it as a potentially warped mirror—and then to measure, and where appropriate to rebalance, that warp.

Start with behaviour rather than principle. Imagine a recruitment pipeline for graduate roles in a London technology firm. Hundreds of candidates apply. CVs are screened, tests administered, interviews conducted. At the end of the process, a familiar pattern emerges: a majority of offers go to men from a small cluster of universities. When the HR director runs the numbers, she notices something more precise. At the initial CV screen, 40 per cent of applicants from underrepresented backgrounds are rejected compared with 20 per cent of others, despite similar qualification levels. At the technical test, pass rates diverge again. By the final stage, the pool is heavily skewed. Show the pattern: diverging pass rates at each gate. Name the mechanism: selection bias embedded in the pipeline. Explain it: historical preferences, informal heuristics, and test designs that advantage some candidates over others produce skew long before "merit" is assessed. The implication is not abstract. Careers are shaped. Teams narrow. Innovation suffers.

The first step in confronting this is brutally simple: measure base rates at each stage. How many people from each group enter? How many progress? Where do they fall away? Base rates are the mirror's outline. Without them, skew remains anecdotal. With them, skew becomes quantifiable. In our London firm, those stage-by-stage numbers expose the specific gates where imbalance appears. Perhaps the technical test filters disproportionately. Perhaps initial CV sifts over-weight certain credentials. Perhaps the final interview panel is homogenous in ways that matter.

A checkable example illustrates this logic at scale. In 2019, the UK Government Equalities Office encouraged employers participating in its gender pay gap reporting scheme to examine recruitment flows, not just salary medians. Several large employers discovered that while starting salaries for men and women in comparable roles were broadly aligned, the pool feeding those roles was not. At one engineering firm, women comprised nearly 40 per cent of applicants but only 15 per cent of hires. Detailed base-rate analysis revealed that women were underrepresented after the first interview round, not at the offer stage. The mirror had previously showed only the final picture. Base-rate measurement revealed where the distortion entered the frame.

A second example, this time from policing, shows the same principle in a different context. In 2017, the UK College of Policing reviewed stop-and-search statistics across several forces. Aggregate data showed disproportionate stops of Black people. When analysts disaggregated by area, time, and officer, they found stark variations: some units applied powers more evenly, others far less so. Base-rate comparisons and outcome analyses (how often searches found prohibited items) allowed forces to identify patterns inconsistent with legitimate targeting. The mirror revealed not just "bias" in general, but specific hotspots where practice diverged from stated aims.

Yet we must acknowledge a counter-example that tempers any sense of easy correction. In 2020, a bank in Europe attempted to rebalance its credit model after discovering that applicants from certain postcodes—correlated with ethnic minority communities—were declined at higher rates. Data scientists introduced fairness constraints and adjusted sampling to reduce disparities. But macroeconomic conditions were shifting, and the historical patterns of default risk were themselves in motion. Some of the corrective adjustments introduced their own instability. Here, the limitation is clear: rebalancing in rapidly changing environments is technically and ethically complex. The mirror keeps moving. The reconciliation lies in humility. Bias mitigation is an ongoing practice, not a one-off fix.

Returning to recruitment—the running example for this subchapter—fairness-aware sampling offers one powerful, pragmatic tool. Once base-rate skews are visible, we can deliberately adjust the way candidates move through the funnel. This does not mean imposing quotas at the end of the process. It means correcting for imbalances at the earlier stages so that assessment has a fair chance to operate.

Imagine that our London firm discovers that candidates from state schools, or from certain ethnic groups, are underrepresented at the interview stage despite comparable test scores. One approach is to implement a "top-up" rule: for each cohort, ensure that a minimum number of candidates from underrepresented backgrounds who meet objective thresholds are advanced, even if they sit just below the arbitrary cut-off that would have been applied globally. This is fairness-aware sampling. It treats the pipeline as a sampling process rather than a perfect meritocracy. It acknowledges that prior filters reflect historical advantage. It re-weights the sample sending people into later stages.

The behaviour changes noticeably. Interview panels now see a more varied slate. Discussions shift. Hiring decisions still focus on capability, but the starting pool is less skewed. Over several cycles, the composition of the workforce begins to reflect a broader slice of qualified applicants rather than the narrow band produced by uncorrected filters.

Some worry that such practices sacrifice "quality". But this anxiety often dissolves when metrics are examined. If underrepresented candidates who meet the same objective bar perform equally well in role—as retention or performance data may show—then fairness-aware sampling has corrected a sampling error, not lowered a standard. The mirror, previously tilted, has been straightened.

Yet we should resist comforting ourselves with technical fixes alone. Bias lives not only in who gets through a funnel, but in what we measure to begin with. If a firm's data records only those candidates who applied, it cannot see those who never did because they perceived the organisation as hostile or unreachable. This is selection bias at the outermost edge. It is visible in behaviour: job adverts placed only in certain networks, career pages showcasing a narrow set of faces, requirements written in ways that assume a particular biography. Data reflecting such a history cannot be neutral. The mirror reflects the room it hangs in.

This is where techniques such as counterfactual analysis and external benchmarking matter. Organisations can compare their applicant pools with external baselines: local labour market data, professional association demographics, university graduate profiles. If the pool diverges sharply—say, drawing disproportionately from a small cluster of institutions or neighbourhoods—that divergence is itself a sign of skew. Measuring who is missing becomes as important as measuring who is present.

Detection, however, is only half the story. Rebalancing requires deliberate choices. Some are structural: changing sourcing channels, rewriting criteria that inadvertently screen out non-traditional candidates, extending outreach to communities previously ignored. Some are algorithmic: adding fairness constraints to models, limiting the influence of historically biased features, monitoring outcomes over time. All require continuous measurement. The mirror must be checked regularly, not glanced at once.

A second named example brings these threads together. In 2016, the law firm Clifford Chance piloted "CV-blind" interviews for some graduate intakes in London. Interviewers did not see university names, focusing instead on competencies and experiences. Later analysis showed that this change, combined with proactive outreach, increased offers to candidates from non-traditional universities. Here, the intervention did not involve high technology or complex models; it adjusted the sampling process and the information fed to human decision-makers. The firm changed the mirror's frame.

Our earlier counter-example—the bank struggling to rebalance its credit model in a shifting economy—reminds us that there are domains where fairness interventions have trade-offs. Adjusting thresholds to equalise approval rates across groups can affect default risk and regulatory compliance. These tensions are real. They cannot be wished away. But naming them explicitly is better than hiding behind claims of neutrality. It allows organisations to engage in informed trade-offs, rather than accidental ones.

Throughout, the motif of the *mirror* returns. Data reflects. It reflects who we have valued, who we have overlooked, what we have chosen to record, and what we have allowed to remain invisible. When we build models or processes on top of that reflection without scrutiny, we risk freezing those patterns into infrastructure. When we measure skew, interrogate base rates, and apply fairness-aware sampling, we begin to polish the glass. We do not erase history. We refuse to mistake it for destiny.

The unresolved tension is not whether bias exists in your data—it does—but what you are prepared to do once you see it. Will you treat the mirror's distortions as unavoidable, a regrettable yet unalterable fact? Or will you accept the discomfort of adjusting your processes, your models, and perhaps your definition of "merit" itself? The forward question is sharp and inescapable: *When the next decision passes through your data pipeline, whose history will it reproduce—and what, concretely, are you willing to change about the mirror it reflects?*

Privacy by Design

In May 2018, the Royal Free London NHS Foundation Trust found itself at the centre of an Information Commissioner's Office ruling after a collaboration with Google DeepMind. The Trust had shared data from 1.6 million patients without sufficient transparency or consent safeguards. The intent was clinical innovation; the outcome was public censure. The ICO concluded that patients "would not have reasonably expected" their data to be used in this way. The incident mattered for more than regulatory reasons. It demonstrated, with painful clarity, that trust is not built on technical sophistication. It is built on restraint. When data collection exceeds what people understand or expect, confidence collapses, and data quality with it.

A smaller, quieter example shows the same lesson in microcosm. In 2021, a community health clinic in Manchester reviewed its intake process after noticing that completion rates on its digital registration form had fallen below 60 per cent. The form had grown bloated over the years: previous managers had added fields "just in case", insurers had requested additional background items, and administrators had appended optional questions that were not truly optional. Patients hesitated. Many abandoned the form. When the clinic stripped it down—removing over a third of the fields, clarifying purpose statements, and adding an automatic expiry for sensitive information—the completion rate rose above 85 per cent within one quarter. Less data gathered, more truth captured. That is the paradox at the heart of privacy by design.

Privacy by design begins with an ethic: *collect only what you truly need*. But it flourishes as a practice: measurable restraint, visible boundaries, and predictable expiry. The motif woven through this subchapter—the *boundary*—captures that discipline. Boundaries define what is collected, how it is used, who sees it, and when it disappears. Without them, data becomes a shapeless resource to be mined endlessly. With them, data becomes a tool: finite, purposeful, and easier for people to trust.

Show the principle in action. A school in Brighton, reviewing its safeguarding processes in 2020, discovered that staff were recording far more personal detail about students than necessary. After a compliance review, the school established a simple rule: if a piece of information was not required for a statutory duty or a defined educational outcome, it would not be collected. Data minimisation was not framed as legal compliance but as a boundary: staff were asked to record the minimum they would need if they had to explain their decision succinctly to a parent. The implication was concrete. Records became sharper, more accurate, and less open to misinterpretation. Privacy did not dilute safeguarding; it strengthened it by removing clutter.

Consider the clinic intake case again. The redesign team began not with the form but with a whiteboard. They listed every task the clinic genuinely needed to perform during a patient's first visit. Then, next to each task, they asked a blunt question: *What single field enables this?* When a field had no corresponding task, it was cut. When a field supported multiple tasks but included sub-questions irrelevant to the core purpose, the sub-questions were retired. The team turned a shapeless form into a boundary: a set of fields each tied to a visible action. The implication was immediate. Staff spent less time validating inconsistent entries. Patients hesitated less because each question had a clear destination.

Minimal collection, however, is only the first boundary. The second is purpose. A dataset without a documented purpose is an invitation to drift. Drift is visible in behaviour: staff accessing records "out of curiosity", analysts rerouting data to explore unrelated correlations, or legacy systems repurposing identifiers for new tools without informed consent. To name a purpose is to prevent drift before it starts. When the UK's Information Commissioner's Office published its guidance on purpose limitation in 2020, the principle at its core was plain: tell people what their data will be used for, and do only that. The implication is not merely ethical. Purpose limits prevent analytical sprawl, reduce operational confusion, and ensure that data collected today does not become a liability during tomorrow's audit.

A second named example reinforces how purpose boundaries shape practice. In 2019, the Norwegian Data Protection Authority reviewed a proposal for a smart-city traffic-monitoring programme in Oslo. Planners wanted to use sensor data to optimise traffic flows. The Authority approved the system on the condition that location data would not be reused for law enforcement, insurance risk assessments, or behavioural profiling. The purpose was narrowly defined. By drawing this boundary at the regulatory stage, Norway ensured that the same dataset could not later be reinterpreted as a surveillance tool. The boundary protected not only privacy but legitimacy.

Yet privacy boundaries face a counter-example that forces nuance. During the first half of 2020, several governments explored digital contact-tracing tools. Some initiatives—such as the decentralised model championed by Apple and Google—adhered closely to privacy-by-design principles: minimal data, local storage, voluntary participation. Others attempted more centralised systems. France's initial StopCovid app, launched in June 2020, drew privacy criticism because the central server processed encounter data in ways that some experts argued created reidentification risks. The limitation here is not that privacy-by-design principles fail during crises, but that urgent public-health needs alter what boundaries are considered legitimate. The reconciliation lies in transparency. Several governments published detailed technical specifications, enabling independent scrutiny and preventing mission creep. Even in exceptions, boundaries existed—because they were argued for in public.

Returning to our motif—the boundary—we can see how expiry policies form a third, equally crucial line. Data without an expiry is data that lingers, often forgotten, in backups, spreadsheets, shared drives, or deprecated systems. It becomes a security risk and a trust hazard. Expiry is a behaviour, not a slogan: deleting stale backups, auto-expiring inactive records, and documenting retention windows in plain language so that staff know what disappears when. A 2022 audit of municipal services in Dublin revealed that systems with automated expiry had 40 per cent fewer access-control issues than those relying on manual deletion. Expiry was not an administrative nicety. It was a trust mechanism.

So how does one integrate expiry into daily practice? The Manchester clinic adopted a simple rule: any sensitive field—sexual health history, substance use disclosures, or domestic context indicators—would automatically expire after a set interval unless explicitly renewed by a clinician with justification. This prevented the silent accumulation of deeply personal data and aligned record-keeping with the clinic's principle of proportionality. The behaviour this created was visible: clinicians paused before opting to retain data, asking whether it remained relevant. That pause—the moment of boundary consciousness—was part of the design.

As we widen the lens, the deeper logic of privacy by design becomes clear. It is not a defensive programme to avoid penalties. It is a method to improve data quality. When people believe you will use their information sparingly, purposefully, and temporarily, they provide more accurate data. Studies conducted by the UK Behavioural Insights Team in 2021 found that participants were significantly more willing to disclose sensitive information when forms displayed concise purpose statements and explicit expiry notices. Trust produced truth. The boundary created clarity.

Still, there is a tension to confront. Some organisations argue that future analytical opportunities justify broad collection now. The logic—"better to have the data in case we need it"—is seductive but flawed. It elevates speculative value above present legitimacy. Yet we cannot deny that innovation sometimes requires flexibility. The reconciliation lies in governance: if data is to be used beyond its original purpose, that extension must be justified, documented, and communicated, with an opt-out where practicable. Boundaries can move, but only with consent.

Throughout, the boundary motif anchors the argument. Minimal fields define which facts you truly need. Purpose limits define what you may do with those facts. Expiry defines how long those facts remain yours. These boundaries are not constraints on innovation. They are conditions for it. Without them, data becomes noise, risk, and suspicion. With them, data becomes cleaner, safer, and more ethically usable.

So the forward test sits here, unresolved: When you next design a form, a database, or a data-sharing protocol, what boundary will you draw first? And if you cannot name that boundary in a sentence clear enough for a sceptical patient, customer, or colleague to understand, what does that say about whether you should collect the data at all?

Explainability for Humans

On 14 March 2022, the Financial Conduct Authority invited representatives from six major lenders to its London office after a wave of complaints about loan-denial letters. The letters were legally compliant. They were also unintelligible. Applicants saw phrases like "adverse credit indicators" and "insufficient affordability alignment" without any explanation of what those terms meant in practice. People appealed decisions they did not understand, phoned call centres for clarification that never arrived, and in some cases lodged formal grievances. When one lender tested a revised letter that translated its criteria into plain language—short sentences, concrete reasons, and a single *because* statement—appeals fell by 22 per cent within two months. Nothing in the underlying scoring model changed. Only the explanation did.

This friction between rules and comprehension is the starting scene of this chapter's argument. A policy can be technically correct and socially brittle. A decision can be fair yet feel opaque. And when people cannot grasp why something happened, they resist—not because they reject the rule, but because the rule never made itself legible. In a world built on procedures, algorithms, and administrative systems, explainability is no longer a courtesy. It is part of the decision itself.

To understand why explainability matters, begin with behaviour. People evaluate rules first by *whether they can follow them*, and only then by *whether they agree with them*. When an explanation lands, behaviour changes: call volumes drop, compliance rises, and the emotional temperature stabilises. This pattern is well documented. In 2017, the Danish Tax Agency published results from an experiment showing that taxpayers were far more likely to correct filing errors when letters highlighted the exact line where the discrepancy appeared. A sentence that named a concrete action—"You did not report income from this employer"—was more effective than any abstract phrasing. The implication was clear: comprehension is a behavioural lever.

The motif threaded through this subchapter—the *lens*—captures what explainability provides. A lens clarifies. It brings the rule into focus. Without a lens, even a well-designed system looks arbitrary from the outside.

A vivid example of this lens in action comes from a debt-policy letter redesign by a regional council in Yorkshire in 2019. Before the redesign, letters informing residents of arrears used stock phrases lifted from statutory templates. Terms such as "priority status" and "means assessment" appeared without context. Behaviour followed the opacity. Residents either ignored the letters or responded with frustration. After a rewrite that included a single sentence explaining the reason—"because your payment has been late three times in the last six weeks"—responses became calmer and earlier. Staff reported fewer confrontational calls. The lens had shifted: the same rule, seen more clearly, became easier to accept.

Explainability is not merely a communication exercise. It is a diagnostic tool. When a rule cannot be explained in plain language, it often indicates that the rule does not make sense even to its designers. This is a recurring lesson in regulatory history. When the Bank of England published its Prudential Regulation Authority guidance in 2016, it encouraged firms to write internal explanations of their own models in accessible English. Many struggled. The difficulty was revealing. The models were less coherent than their technical gloss implied. The implication is sharp: if an organisation cannot explain how a decision works, the problem may lie in the decision, not the explanation.

Yet explainability also faces genuine limits. Complex systems—credit models, diagnostic algorithms, security protocols—cannot always be fully reduced to a few sentences without distortion. A counter-example shows this tension. When the US Social Security Administration attempted to simplify its disability-benefit denial notices in 2014, early drafts removed so much detail that applicants could not discern the medical rationale. Appeals surged. The reconciliation lies in balance. Brevity is not the goal. Comprehensibility is. A clear explanation may be short or long, but it must map directly to the criteria that drove the decision.

The recruitment pipeline offers a practical arena in which to observe how explainability disciplines design. When a London-based software firm reviewed its hiring process in 2020, it discovered that candidates frequently asked why they had failed at the technical-test stage. The firm's existing explanation—"benchmark misalignment"—meant nothing. After an internal audit, hiring leads rewrote their communication to reference *specific* signals: incomplete logic paths, inconsistent variable naming, or failure to meet a timed requirement. The firm also introduced fairness-aware sampling and published its stage-by-stage base rates. Candidates reported higher perceptions of fairness even when rejected. The explanation did not soften the disappointment, but it restored a sense of procedural dignity.

This connection between dignity and explanation appears again in public services. In 2015, the New South Wales Ombudsman reviewed complaint data from social-housing tenants. A pattern emerged. Tenants who understood the reason for a decision—allocation delays, eligibility thresholds, maintenance prioritisation—were less likely to escalate their complaints. Explainability functioned as a pressure valve. When the Ombudsman recommended rewriting standard letters to emphasise because statements tied to observable criteria, housing authorities reported improved compliance and fewer hostile interactions. Again, the lens clarified the rule without weakening it.

Explainability is also a safeguard against discriminatory drift. When people can see the criteria, they can question them. When the criteria remain opaque, bias hides. A 2021 review by the UK Race Disparity Unit illustrated this point with school behavioural sanctions. Schools that published simple rationales for decisions—linking sanctions to named behaviours rather than ambiguous categories—saw fewer group-based disparities. Opacity, by contrast, correlated with inconsistent enforcement. Making the rationale visible created accountability, not fragility.

Still, the demand for clarity must not collapse into oversimplification. Some rules contain nuance that cannot be eliminated without harm. Refugee-status determinations, forensic assessments, and safeguarding decisions require contextual judgement. A credible limitation arises here. Overly reductive explanations may give false confidence or misrepresent complexity. Reconciling this requires a tiered approach: a primary explanation written in plain language, accompanied by an optional deeper layer for those who need it. The lens can have multiple depths of focus.

Throughout these examples, the pattern repeats. Show the decision. Name the criterion. Explain the reason. Observe the behaviour that follows. Each step reflects the central truth that human acceptance depends not on liking the rule but on *seeing* it.

The lens motif returns once more in the form of an unresolved question. When organisations next draft a policy letter, publish model criteria, or release an automated decision, what lens will they offer the people affected? A blurred one that obscures the logic? Or a clear one that allows them to understand, respond, and, if necessary, contest the outcome?

The test is simple to state and difficult to meet: *Could a person outside your system repeat the reason for your decision in one sentence?* If not, the rule may function—but it does not yet explain itself.

Chapter 5
Time, Attention, and Decision Flow

The moment that finally broke the spell arrived on a damp Tuesday morning in February 2020. A product team at a London fintech company, exhausted by months of unstructured decision-making, gathered for yet another emergency review. The issue was trivial—an approval for a marketing spend so small it could have been settled in minutes—but it had bounced between Slack threads, late-night emails, and four different calendars before landing here. "We're not short of talent," the director observed, looking around the room. "We're short of rhythm." That meeting produced a simple experiment: all such approvals would move to a twice-weekly decision board. Within a fortnight the churn collapsed. The team had not changed its competence. It had changed its cadence.

Timing seems banal until it becomes the failure point. Decisions rarely fall apart because the humans making them are incapable; they fall apart because the flow of work is fractured, attention scattered, and the organisation's pulse undefined. A decision made at the wrong moment can be every bit as flawed as a decision made with the wrong data. Yet rhythm is invisible. Unlike budgets or strategies or KPI dashboards, cadence has no dedicated owner. It governs everything and belongs to no one. That invisibility makes it powerful, and dangerous, in equal measure.

Modern work cultures elevate responsiveness as a virtue, yet the cost is unmistakable: teams trapped in a perpetual now, reacting rather than deciding, mistaking speed for flow and noise for urgency. The truth is older and simpler. Humans are temporal creatures. We think better when events are paced, when similar decisions are batched, when attention is protected, and when the irreversible is separated from the easily undone. Machine systems formalise this through queues, schedules, and priority flags. Humans often rely on improvisation. This chapter proposes a reconciliation. Time can be shaped deliberately, not endured.

Consider the structures already around us that hint at forgotten wisdom: courtrooms that follow fixed session times; academic timetables that anchor thinking to recurring cycles; surgical lists that batch similar procedures to reduce errors. These domains evolved patterns that recognise cognitive limits. High-stakes decisions require rhythm. But in many organisations—particularly knowledge-intensive ones—the calendar has become an ungoverned territory: overfilled, underthought, treated as a receptacle rather than a design space. The calendar looks neutral. It is not. It is an algorithm, silently computing whose time matters, whose attention fragments, and which decisions are made well or badly.

This chapter argues that decision quality is a temporal achievement. Choices are rarely isolated. They live within flows of information, expectations, and interruptions. To design decisions is to design the architecture around them. And that architecture, more than any tool or model, determines whether an organisation acts with coherence or clatter.

The first building block is batching. When similar decisions accumulate and are handled together, the mind works with comparative clarity. Patterns emerge. Trade-offs become visible. Emotional temperature stabilises. The fintech team discovered this when they moved their approvals to set days: decisions became faster because decision-makers were present, focused, and primed. The paradox is that slowing the *timing* of choices often accelerates the *speed* of execution. Rhythm creates efficiency.

The second block is escalation discipline. Too many organisations escalate by default, not by exception. A manager's calendar becomes a holding tank for unresolved judgements that should have been settled earlier, lower, or not at all. Escalation by exception reverses this logic. Only predefined triggers—threshold breaches, risk flags, ambiguity beyond a set boundary—should summon higher authority. This frees leaders for deep work and restores autonomy to teams. It also forces organisations to articulate what truly warrants attention. Silence becomes a signal, not a vacuum.

Then comes the calendar itself, a contested territory masquerading as a neutral tool. A calendar with no defaults is a calendar shaped by other people's urgency. The introduction of protected morning blocks, meeting-free afternoons, or weekly recovery space does not simply reorganise time; it reorganises thought. When one consultancy firm in Edinburgh guarded its mornings for deep project work, project throughput increased—not because staff worked longer hours, but because they worked undisturbed. The firm had not discovered productivity. It had rediscovered sovereignty over attention.

Finally, reversibility alters the emotional climate of decision-making. When teams distinguish between reversible and irreversible choices, fear diminishes. Kill switches—explicit rollback mechanisms—turn experimentation from bravado into method. A pricing test released with a rollback plan is not a gamble; it is a controlled exploration. Machine systems have long benefited from safe-fail mechanisms. Human systems often default to caution because failure is final. Reversibility repositions failure as feedback.

Threaded through each of these elements is a motif: *flow*. Not the romanticised flow of creativity, but the engineered flow of systems thinking—a state in which decisions move smoothly, queues are intentional, and interruptions have meaning. Flow is not a luxury. It is a foundation for clarity.

The significance of time design reaches beyond productivity. It shapes fairness. When decisions are rushed, the loudest voices prevail. When decisions are scattered across arbitrary moments, those with the most flexible schedules exert disproportionate influence. Rhythm redistributes power. Cadence creates equality.

There is also a moral dimension. Attention is not an infinite resource. It is a social good. When organisations squander it—through poorly timed requests, incessant context shifts, or perpetual near-termism—they exhaust not just individuals but collective judgement. Designing time is designing care.

As we turn deeper into the chapter, the questions sharpen. How do we choose the right cadence for different classes of decisions? How do we craft exception triggers that protect leadership attention without trapping information? What does a well-designed calendar reveal about an organisation's values, not just its operations? How do kill switches change the psychology of risk? And perhaps most provocatively: what would your decisions look like if your organisation treated time as method rather than backdrop?

The promise ahead is practical and philosophical. Practical, because you will learn techniques to structure daily, weekly, and quarterly decision cycles; to build exception protocols; to repair calendars; and to embed reversible decisions. Philosophical, because beneath these techniques lies a deeper provocation: time is not merely the medium through which decisions pass. It is the material from which good decisions are made.

The chapter opens the door to a reimagined organisational rhythm—a tempo that steadies attention, clarifies choices, and enables teams to think with the grace and precision of well-designed systems. The next step is yours.

Batching and Cadence

At 09:12 on 4 February 2020, in a glass-walled meeting room at HelixPay's Shoreditch office, product director Maya Rahman opened her laptop to a spreadsheet that embarrassed the entire team. It listed every "urgent" approval she had given in the previous month: forty-seven in total, scattered across Slack messages, ad-hoc calls, late-night emails, and hastily convened stand-ups. Each item, taken alone, was trivial—a £900 design contract, a short extension to a beta test, a modest revision to a marketing budget. Together, they formed a picture of chronic dysfunction. Decisions were happening everywhere and nowhere. When HelixPay replaced this chaos with a twice-weekly approval board, the volume of interruptions fell by more than half by the end of March. The work had not changed. The *timing* had.

This scene is a quiet but telling example of something most organisations sense but rarely articulate. Decisions do not merely require judgement; they require rhythm. A good decision at a bad moment is a bad decision in disguise. A team overwhelmed by asynchronous requests operates in permanent reaction. The texture of work becomes jittery. Attention splinters. People begin to treat their calendars as emergency rooms, not as tools. Cadence—the sequencing and clustering of decisions—often determines whether a group can think at all. Yet cadence is so mundane, so woven into the background, that leaders rarely name it. They feel its absence as frustration, not as design failure.

The motif that threads through this subchapter—the *pulse*—helps illuminate the issue. A healthy system has a discernible pulse. Its rhythms give shape to the day, the week, the quarter. They tell people when to act, when to pause, when to escalate, and when to hold steady. HelixPay had no pulse until it built one. And once it did, decision quality rose not because people became wiser, but because they became synchronised.

To understand why batching improves judgement, start with the behaviour itself. When decisions are grouped, comparison emerges. Seeing several similar requests side by side exposes patterns: duplicated work, strategic misalignment, hidden risks, repeated justifications. Batching is not an efficiency trick; it is a cognitive scaffold. It enables a team to see the contours of its thinking. When HelixPay reviewed five to ten approvals together, the discussions shifted from isolated debates ("Should we approve this change?") to structural ones ("Why are we receiving so many of this kind of request?"). Batching created a higher vantage point.

This pattern has historical precedent. In 1816, the Admiralty in London introduced scheduled review days for naval procurement, replacing ad-hoc visits from suppliers. The change reduced fraudulent submissions and improved record-keeping. Naming the specific practice—cadenced procurement—allowed historians to trace how regularity fostered better oversight. The implication is that even in early bureaucratic systems, cadence was a form of governance.

A second named example comes from Toyota's production system in Aichi Prefecture during the early 1970s. Contrary to later mythologisation, Toyota did not operate at breakneck speed. It operated at rhythm. Line managers reviewed small but recurring operational decisions during fixed "hansei" cycles. This predictability enabled teams to surface problems consistently and prevented panic-driven improvisation. The cadence did not slow innovation. It steadied it.

The pulse motif also helps explain why unbatched decisions feel so costly. Interruptions are not neutral. They impose measurable switching costs. In 2008, researchers at UC Irvine quantified the average recovery time after an interruption at over 20 minutes. That metric, widely cited and often misunderstood, describes attention, not etiquette. Every unstructured decision request drains the cognitive reservoir. A leadership team making dozens of tiny, poorly timed judgements each day is like a heart beating irregularly—too fast, too scattered, unable to push blood with force.

But cadence faces a credible limitation, and a counter-example helps sharpen it. During emergencies, batching can slow responses unacceptably. In March 2020, during the early weeks of the pandemic, several NHS Trusts discovered that previously batched processes—procurement approvals, rota adjustments, clinical policy reviews—had to shift into continuous flow. Delays cost lives. The limitation is real: cadence must match context. The reconciliation lies not in abandoning batching, but in distinguishing *operational urgency* from *organisational habit*. HelixPay's approvals were not emergencies. They felt urgent only because the system had lost its pulse. Where the stakes are immediate and high, cadence compresses; where stakes are moderate and sustained, cadence expands.

The strength of batching lies not only in weekly rhythms but in daily and quarterly ones. Daily rhythms shape attention. Morning focus windows, mid-day huddles, evening audits—each stands as a micro-pulse that directs cognitive energy. Weekly rhythms gather related decisions. Quarterly rhythms provide altitude: strategic reviews, resource allocation, course corrections. When these cycles align, organisations develop a sense of temporal coherence. People know when decisions will be made, when voices will be heard, and when silence signals consensus rather than neglect.

The recruitment pipeline is one domain where cadence quietly reshapes fairness. A firm in Manchester discovered in 2019 that candidate evaluations were wildly inconsistent across the week. Monday reviews were exceptionally strict; Friday reviews were lenient. The firm shifted to twice-weekly evaluation panels. Evaluations stabilised. The behaviour changed because the pulse changed. Cadence moderated variance.

Yet even this can go too far. If every decision is batched, opportunities are missed. A marketing team that waits two weeks to approve a social-media response plan will underperform competitors. A hospital that batches triage decisions would be reckless. The counter-example underscores a principle: batching is a design choice, not an ideology. It should cluster what benefits from comparison and flow, not what requires immediacy. To reconcile this, organisations must build a taxonomy of decision types. Some decisions demand rhythm; others demand immediacy. The pulse must be adaptable.

Returning to HelixPay, the change that seemed small—a twice-weekly approval board—reconfigured the team's sense of time. The chatter of asynchronous requests faded. Slack channels calmed. People worked with fewer interruptions. Managers regained deep-work hours. But the transformation was deeper than productivity. The team no longer mistook noise for urgency. They built temporal boundaries and defended them.

This raises a broader implication. Cadence does not merely support efficiency. It enforces discernment. When decisions have scheduled homes, people ask themselves a quiet but vital question: *Does this need to happen now?* That pause is the hallmark of mature judgement. It is the difference between a system reacting to stimuli and a system acting by design.

Threading back to our motif, the pulse reminds us that organisations are living systems. When the pulse is erratic, everything feels frantic. When the pulse is steady, clarity returns. Time becomes an ally rather than an adversary.

The unresolved question sits at the end of this subchapter like a diagnostic tool: Which decisions in your organisation deserve a pulse, and which have been allowed to hijack attention simply because no one imposed a rhythm? And if you mapped all the interruptions, requests, and approvals of your past week onto a single page, would you recognise a cadence—or only noise?

Escalate by Exception

At 08:47 on 16 September 2019, at the headquarters of NorthStar Logistics in Birmingham, operations director Helen O'Donnell opened her calendar and saw the week's pattern with a clarity that felt accusatory. Every day was clogged with meetings triggered by minor decisions: a supplier invoice marginally above forecast, a delivery route adjustment, a customer credit limit query. None of them merited senior attention. Yet all had found their way to her desk because the company had evolved a culture where escalation was habitual rather than exceptional. When NorthStar introduced a simple threshold system the following month—codifying which conditions *must* rise to O'Donnell and which must not—her meeting load fell by 40 per cent by December. The lesson was immediate. Leadership had not been suffering from too many decisions. It had been suffering from undifferentiated ones.

This experience reflects a broader truth that many organisations already feel in their bones: people escalate because they lack boundaries, not because they lack confidence. Without a defined structure, uncertainty travels upwards by default, collecting managers like debris in a rising tide. The result is a landscape of unnecessary meetings, delayed progress, and leaders who spend their best cognitive hours adjudicating issues that should have been resolved two layers below. Escalation, when undefined, becomes the organisational equivalent of background noise—ever-present, distracting, and silently corrosive.

The motif woven through this subchapter—the *signal*—captures what escalation should be. A signal is specific. It arises only when conditions demand attention. It stands out precisely because everything else stays quiet. In healthy systems, escalation is a signal. In unhealthy ones, it is static.

To see how the signal model works in practice, consider NorthStar's intervention. The company defined explicit exceptions: any delivery deviation exceeding 20 minutes, any invoice variance above 10 per cent, any customer complaint involving safety concerns. Everything else stayed local. By naming the exceptions, NorthStar created a shared mental model. Team leaders could act autonomously because they knew when autonomy ended. Managers could reclaim deep work because their time was no longer held hostage by trivialities. The signal became audible.

This logic has historical precedent. In 1969, NASA revised its mission control procedures after investigating near-miss communication failures during Apollo 10. Instead of constant cross-channel updates, the agency moved towards an exception-based reporting structure. Flight controllers relayed information only when telemetry crossed defined thresholds or when anomalies appeared. Naming the pattern—exception-based reporting—transformed the culture of decision flow. The implication was powerful: clarity does not arise from more communication, but from *better-shaped* communication.

A second, more contemporary example comes from a 2018 review of digital operations at GOV.UK Notify. The platform team noticed that engineers were being interrupted dozens of times each day for clarification requests about non-critical notifications. By late summer, they introduced a flagged escalation protocol: only incidents breaching uptime thresholds or affecting a minimum number of users triggered direct engineer involvement. Everything else entered an asynchronous queue. Within two months, engineers regained several hours of uninterrupted focus each week. Productivity rose because the signal was sharpened.

But exception-based escalation faces a credible limitation, and a counter-example illustrates it. During the 2021 summer floods in Germany, several regional agencies used thresholded alert systems to escalate flood warnings. Some thresholds were too rigid. By the time conditions crossed the defined limits, communities had already lost evacuation windows. The limitation is clear: in crisis contexts, strict thresholds may lag reality. The reconciliation is likewise clear. Exception systems must be revisited regularly and must make room for domain expertise—allowing professionals to escalate based on informed judgement even when metrics remain below trigger points. A signal must be sensitive, not blind.

Returning to everyday organisational life, the power of exception-based escalation lies partly in the behaviours it creates. When teams know they are responsible for decisions beneath a threshold, they prepare better. They gather relevant information, consult colleagues, compare precedents. This behaviour reinforces trust. It gives autonomy contour. And trust, when measured not as sentiment but as visible action—the speed at which decisions are made, the willingness to own outcomes, the reduction in reflexive forwarding—becomes a metric of organisational health.

The signal motif reappears when examining calendar behaviour. Managers in escalation-heavy environments behave as though their diaries belong to everyone else. Meetings appear like intrusions, crowding out strategic work. But once exceptions are defined, the calendar changes shape. In the first month of NorthStar's threshold system, O'Donnell blocked three mornings per week for uninterrupted strategic planning. The behaviour shift was immediate: teams stopped "just checking" small decisions because the signal had been codified. Silence became meaningful.

Exception systems also change power dynamics. When escalation is routine, decision-making concentrates at the top. When escalation is triggered only by defined conditions, decision-making decentralises. Team members learn that they are trusted to act within boundaries. This has measurable effects. Research published by the Centre for Evidence-Based Management in 2019 found that teams with clear decision-boundaries had 30–40 per cent fewer approval delays than those with ambiguous escalation norms. These are behavioural data points, not abstractions.

Yet exception systems require maintenance. Thresholds drift. Organisations evolve. What was once an exception may become routine. A credible warning emerges here: exception-based escalation can calcify if it is not reviewed. The remedy is rhythm. Quarterly reviews of threshold logic allow organisations to recalibrate. The signal must adapt to the environment.

Across industries—aviation, finance, healthcare, digital operations—exception-based escalation reveals a consistent pattern: clarity liberates attention. When the signal is clear, the mind steadies. Decisions no longer arrive in a shapeless torrent. They arrive as shaped events, each with a place in the system.

But a final, unresolved question remains—the forward test that determines whether an organisation has built a system of signals or merely a new layer of bureaucracy: *What, exactly, deserves to interrupt you?* If a team cannot answer that in a single, specific sentence, then escalation remains static rather than signal, and leaders will continue to drown in meetings convened not because they are necessary, but because no one has defined when they are not.

Designing Good Defaults in Calendars

At 09:12 on 3 February 2020, at the London offices of Hargreaves Lansdown, head of product development Priya Desai noticed something unsettling in her weekly performance review. Across eight teams, project throughput—the number of deliverables completed to specification within the sprint window—had dropped almost 25 per cent compared with the previous quarter. Yet hours worked had risen. The culprit emerged in a single diagnostic chart: meetings had expanded to fill the mornings, crowding into what developers repeatedly identified as their highest-clarity hours. Within a month, Desai introduced a simple intervention. Mornings, 09:00–12:00, became default protected blocks for focused work. Meetings shifted to afternoons unless explicitly justified. By May 2020, throughput had recovered and then exceeded its earlier peak. The calendar, not the talent, had been the problem.

That moment crystallised a truth too often overlooked: calendars act like silent algorithms. They compute, constrain, and channel decisions long before any individual decides what to do. A blank calendar looks neutral, yet its emptiness invites intrusion. A populated one looks intentional, even when its entries result not from preference but from drift. Defaults—the pre-set conditions that shape behaviour before choices are made—decide far more than intention alone. In Desai's case, team leads had not chosen to sacrifice mornings. They had simply never protected them.

That silence—the calendar's quiet logic—is the motif that runs through this piece. Silence can guard cognition or drain it. It depends on what the system assumes when you are not looking.

A good default shifts the burden of proof. Instead of asking why a meeting should be protected time, the default asks why it should invade protected time. The difference is subtle yet consequential. The former places the defence on the individual; the latter places it on the requester. To understand why this matters, we turn to the broader architecture of behavioural design: when friction lies in the path of the lower-value choice rather than the higher-value one, behaviour changes predictably and sustainably.

The idea that default structures outperform ad-hoc scheduling has historical precedent. In 2009, the UK Cabinet Office tested default meeting-free Fridays for several policy teams at 70 Whitehall. The pilot, documented in internal productivity memos later released under FOI, showed an increase in completed policy drafts of around 15 per cent over eight weeks. The explanation was mundane yet revelatory: uninterrupted mornings accumulated into uninterrupted days; uninterrupted days allowed deep analysis; deep analysis produced better drafts. The default did the work.

A second example, this time from 2016 at MIT's Sloan School of Management, illustrates the same principle in an academic environment. Several research groups adopted a shared calendar protocol: no meetings before 11:00 unless they involved external collaborators constrained by time zones. The teams monitored three metrics—paper submission rates, revision turnaround times, and grant-proposal quality scores. Submission rates rose modestly, but revision times improved significantly. Scholars attributed the improvement to the protected cognitive window in which they could return to complex models or messy datasets without interruption. Here again, silence became a structural asset.

But defaults have limits, and a credible counter-example shows where they may falter. In early 2022, a Scandinavian fintech attempted to enforce a universal "focus-only morning" rule across engineering, sales, and customer support. Within weeks, escalation backlogs grew in support, and client response times deteriorated. A rigid default had collided with a domain whose demands were inherently time-sensitive. The reconciliation is instructive: good defaults must honour task variability. They cannot be uniform impositions; they must adapt to the rhythms of each function. A support team lives inside real-time volatility; their mornings cannot be sealed off in the same way as a research team's. The default must fit the work.

Returning to Desai's case, the behavioural shift was measurable. Developers reported fewer context switches, measured by a simple internal metric: the number of task changes recorded per day in the version-control system. That figure dropped from an average of nine per day to six. The impact on perceived autonomy was equally clear. In post-intervention interviews, several developers noted that they no longer had to "defend" their mornings. The system defended them. Trust—visible here as a reduction in defensive behaviours—rose because the calendar had been designed to respect attention rather than confiscate it.

The power of good defaults rests partly in their ability to expose hidden choices. When a calendar is open, saying yes feels costless; when time is blocked, every yes feels like a conscious override. Override is a diagnostic behaviour. It forces a meeting requester to articulate value. It forces a participant to measure opportunity cost. In organisational environments, articulated value is rare. Defaults make it necessary.

The silence motif returns here. A calendar with good defaults produces a kind of structured silence, an intentional quiet in which deep work can take root. But silence must be maintained. A calendar erodes unless tended. New initiatives creep into mornings "just this once." Emergency meetings become routine. Leaders must review defaults quarterly, much like engineers review safety thresholds, to ensure drift does not rewrite the system.

Another implication emerges from the interplay between defaults and culture. Defaults signal norms. When a firm protects mornings, it tells staff that concentration is valued. When afternoons cluster with meetings, it signals that collaboration is structured rather than chaotic. These signals shape identity. Organisations become predictable environments rather than theatres of constant interruption.

Yet another example strengthens the case. In 2014, the London-based design studio Berg introduced a rule: no internal meetings between 10:00 and 13:00 during prototyping phases. While the studio closed the following year, interviews with former staff published in *Creative Review* noted that during the rule's active period, prototypes progressed more quickly because designers had a protected stretch for iterative exploration. Even in creative contexts, where spontaneity is prized, default protections served as scaffolding for invention.

Still, defaults must coexist with reversibility. A well-designed calendar allows overrides when necessary, and these overrides must be easy to revert. The ethic is simple: firm defaults, flexible adjustments. This principle protects against rigidity while preserving structure. It also ensures that defaults remain tools rather than constraints.

As calibration instruments, calendars shape day-to-day energy expenditure. Default recovery blocks—short intervals where no meetings can be scheduled—help prevent the slow accumulation of cognitive debt. Cognitive debt is visible in small behaviours: the delayed response to emails, the gradual decline in creative contribution, the shrinking willingness to take on risk. When a calendar protects recovery, these behaviours change. Metrics such as response times and cycle times recover alongside human stamina.

This interplay between recovery and focus highlights a final insight: high-performance environments are environments of rhythm. Rhythm emerges from structure. Structure emerges from defaults.

The unresolved tension lies here: if calendars behave as silent algorithms, who writes their code? If you do not choose your defaults, someone else's urgency will choose them for you. The test for any team or leader is stark. Are your mornings shaped by intention, or by intrusion? Only one of these paths leads to more meaningful work.

Kill Switches and Reversibility

At 08:47 on 12 September 2019, at the headquarters of Monzo Bank in London, product manager Elena Venkova authorised a pricing experiment she had hesitated over for weeks. The proposal was simple: adjust the overdraft fee structure for a randomly selected 5 per cent of active current accounts. Analysts projected the test would expose potential revenue gains but risk a measurable dip in customer sentiment. The tension was classic—promise against peril, learning against loyalty. What broke the deadlock was not better forecasting, but a device built into the decision itself: a kill switch. If customer complaints exceeded a narrow tolerance band within 72 hours, the test would automatically roll back to the prior pricing schedule. That switch made speed possible. The experiment launched before noon. By the following afternoon, with complaint volumes within safe limits and transaction behaviour stable, the team expanded the cohort. The kill switch had made a risky choice reversible, and reversibility had made it fast.

Reversible decisions behave differently. They reward action. Irreversible decisions punish error. Organisations that cannot distinguish between the two tend to treat every choice as if it carried permanent consequences. They slow down not because the work is complex but because the stakes are inflated. Decisions accumulate waiting time. Meetings multiply. Momentum evaporates. Venkova's intervention demonstrated the alternative: engineer the boundary between reversible and irreversible, and use that boundary to restore decisiveness.

Reversibility, however, is not merely a label; it is a structural property. A decision is reversible when the system around it allows rollback without damaging trust, eroding safety, or destroying value. The motif that threads through this analysis—the switch—is both literal and conceptual. A kill switch works because it enforces humility: it assumes failure is possible and designs for it.

The logic became clearer during Amazon's 2004 service-pricing reform, documented in internal memos later cited in Brad Stone's *The Everything Store*. Senior engineers categorised proposals into "Type 1" (irreversible) and "Type 2" (reversible) decisions. Type 2 decisions moved quickly. Teams were encouraged to experiment, monitor, and revert. That taxonomy, simple as it was, helped reduce cycle times for smaller product changes. This example teaches a crucial point: classification clarifies pace. When a team knows what kind of decision it is making, it knows how fast it may proceed.

Another case strengthens the lesson. In 2018, Transport for London tested a small alteration to the frequency schedule for southbound buses on Route 436 during morning peak hours. The target was to ease congestion between Deptford and Peckham by shifting three departures by a margin of four minutes each. The trial, documented in TfL's publicly released operations report, ran for two weeks with a reversal trigger: if average passenger wait times increased by more than 40 seconds at any stop, the schedule would revert overnight. The trial succeeded, reducing bus bunching without breaching the wait-time threshold. The reversible nature of the change—predefined metrics, automatic rollback, no structural reconfiguration—enabled TfL to test a risk that would otherwise have demanded months of modelling. The presence of a kill switch shifted the decision from a brittle commitment to a flexible probe.

Kill switches do not eliminate risk. They regulate it. They transform the consequences of error by preventing escalation. A credible counter-example shows their limits. In 2021, a European retail chain attempted a reversible pricing pilot across ten stores, adjusting promotional discounts for high-volume items. Although the change was labelled reversible, the stores lacked real-time price update systems. Reverting the prices required manual intervention across hundreds of shelf labels and digital displays. The "reversal" took four days, during which customer confusion and staff workload spiked. The lesson is sharp: reversibility must be operational, not merely conceptual. A kill switch must actually switch.

The implication extends beyond operations into culture. Teams trust reversible decisions because they experience the reversals. The behaviour matters. When employees see a change rolled back promptly after crossing a threshold—whether complaints, product defects, or safety signals—they learn that leadership honours data over ego. That builds a form of grounded trust visible in how people escalate concerns, how candidly they report anomalies, and how willing they are to initiate small experiments.

Metrics make kill switches work. Without clear thresholds, a switch becomes a slogan. In Venkova's Monzo trial, the team monitored two indicators: daily complaint volume and net promoter score for affected customers. Both had precise tolerances. In the TfL example, the 40-second limit made the decision crisp. Thresholds direct attention; they remove ambiguity. Ambiguity is what slows teams down.

The motif of the switch returns here. A switch divides states: on/off, go/stop, continue/revert. This binary quality forces clarity in an organisational context that often encourages vagueness. Clarity is not just intellectual; it is behavioural. When people know the moment at which a system will pull back, they commit more fully to moving forward.

That said, kill switches introduce their own tension. They create speed but invite overuse. Leaders may be tempted to declare every significant move reversible simply to accelerate approval. That temptation must be resisted. Not all decisions tolerate reversal. Contract renegotiations, public safety communications, mergers, and regulatory commitments often carry irreversible reputational and legal consequences. The reconciliation lies in accurate classification. Treat reversible decisions as experiments and irreversible decisions as designs.

One can see this distinction in the FDA's drug-recall protocols in the United States, where reversible distribution halts differ sharply from irreversible market withdrawals. The former can be executed swiftly; the latter require extensive documentation, legal consultation, and coordinated public statements. Each path has different latency and different risk. The distinction is structural, not merely terminological.

Returning to product development, reversible decisions create an iterative rhythm. A team that knows it can reverse a feature will release earlier, measure earlier, and learn earlier. The opposite rhythm—debate, refine, re-debate—signals fear of consequences. The reversible mindset counteracts that stagnation.

A point about data closes the loop. Kill switches depend on high-frequency monitoring. A pricing test that checks metrics monthly is not reversible in practice. A feature launch that requires manual analysis across ten spreadsheets cannot safely be rolled back in minutes. The monitoring system itself must be designed for reversibility: real-time dashboards, automated alerts, clear timestamps. Without measurement, a switch is blind.

The unresolved tension that concludes this discussion is this: which decisions in your environment masquerade as irreversible only because no one has built the mechanisms that would make them reversible? How many choices sit dormant behind the illusion of permanence? And if you could install one kill switch tomorrow—a single thresholded reversal that would allow your organisation to learn faster—where would you place it?

Chapter 6
Ethics as a Feature

The call came just after dawn, when the distribution yard in Rotterdam was still half-lit by the orange spill from the harbour cranes. A senior planner at a European delivery firm—one of those quiet operators who keep the continent's commercial bloodstream moving—had uncovered a route optimisation that promised a seven-figure annual saving. The path was elegant on a map: a tight, efficient arc around the city's eastern fringe, cutting distance, time, and fuel. Yet the route threaded through a residential corridor where cyclists and heavy lorries had collided twice that spring. The algorithm saw only minutes saved; the planners saw the kind of risk that leaves more than spreadsheets dented. Within hours, the leadership team overrode the optimisation and locked that corridor out of future planning runs. Profit yielded to principle, not because the numbers were wrong, but because numbers alone cannot carry the weight of a life. It was a small decision with a large truth embedded: ethics is not an afterthought. It is a design choice.

That tension—between measurable gain and moral constraint—sits at the heart of modern decision-making. The more precisely we optimise, the more clearly we see the trade-offs that optimisation conceals. A model that performs well on historical data may unintentionally encode the very inequities a society wants to move beyond. A rule that distributes scarce resources may do so efficiently while failing a particular family, neighbourhood, or edge case. Efficiency without judgement is a brittle virtue. It performs beautifully until the moment it matters most. The question is not whether we will make decisions using metrics, but whether those metrics will live within boundaries shaped by human values rather than brute calculation.

The systems we build—whether routing engines, allocation tools, risk scores, or service rules—carry assumptions about fairness, dignity, and harm. Those assumptions matter because the people governed by such systems feel their consequences directly. A tenant waiting for housing allocation does not experience a model; they experience the waiting. A shop manager whose transaction is flagged as fraudulent experiences not the statistical threshold but the implication that their integrity requires further checking. When rules are opaque or inflexible, people resist them. When they are transparent, principled, and proportionate, people may accept outcomes they dislike because they can see the path by which those outcomes were reached.

This chapter traces the architecture of ethical decision-making in a world saturated with data and algorithms. It argues that ethics functions best not as decoration or compliance but as a feature—designed, engineered, and tested with the same discipline we apply to performance or reliability. That shift in perspective changes the work. Instead of treating dilemmas as exceptional events to be escalated, we design systems that anticipate them, surface them early, and handle them with clarity and care.

We begin with principled overrides: the structured way an organisation declares its non-negotiables. These are the compact truths that shape action when metrics pull in the wrong direction. The Rotterdam example sits in this category. A company that chooses safety over margin signals the boundaries of its identity. Overrides of this sort do not slow an organisation down; they prevent it from drifting into patterns that erode trust or incur hidden liabilities. But an override only works if the principles are known in advance, not improvised in crisis.

From there, we examine the discipline of harm anticipation. The most successful designers of rules imagine failure before it arrives. They conduct structured pre-mortems, asking who could be harmed, how, and under what conditions. It is an ancient habit with a modern register. Roman engineers, as chronicled by Vitruvius in the first century BCE, were required to walk beneath the arches they designed; their personal risk ensured diligence. Our version is less visceral but no less necessary. Consider a housing allocation rule that treats all households as identical units. Stress-testing that rule against the lived complexity of larger families reveals where it may fracture. Ethics here is foresight.

Yet foresight alone does not sustain legitimacy. People accept difficult outcomes if the process is visibly fair. That is where proportionality and due process enter. It is not the presence of tough criteria that erodes trust; it is the absence of a path for appeal, explanation, or human review. A fraud detection system that rejects applications outright generates anger and suspicion. The same system, when it flags cases for a secondary human check, demonstrates respect. A rule can be stern without being harsh.

Documentation provides the last structural layer. Reasoning that is not recorded is reasoning that cannot be audited, explained, or improved. A simple log—a date, a rationale, the data consulted, the constraints considered—does more than defend decisions; it teaches. Mistakes become assets. They reveal where assumptions were misplaced, where incentives distorted behaviour, where harm slipped through a gap no one had mapped. Over time, a culture that records decisions becomes a culture that learns from them.

Across these sections runs a quiet motif: the ledger. Every decision writes to it. Some entries reflect clear trade-offs; others reveal emergent patterns of inequity or risk. The ledger does not serve judgement in a moralistic sense; it serves memory. And memory is what prevents organisations from repeating the same ethical mistakes under slightly different guises.

The stakes are not abstract. As machine learning systems grow more capable, they invite delegation. Delegation without design creates distance between action and accountability. That distance is hazardous. An automated decision that harms someone with no channel for redress, no record of reasoning, and no human oversight is not simply an operational failure. It is a moral one. Bringing ethics into the design of decisions closes that distance. It restores proportion, transparency, and agency.

Yet a paradox lingers beneath this work: too much caution paralyses. Too little caution injures. Navigating that tension requires an approach that is neither cynical about rules nor naive about constraints. It requires tools that allow teams to move fast without moving blindly. Principles that can withstand pressure. Stress-tests that reveal fragility. Pathways that ensure fairness. Logs that ensure accountability. All of these combine into a system that is both humane and operationally resilient.

As you move forward, consider the unsettled questions that animate this chapter. How do we design rules that protect without patronising? How do we encode non-negotiables without ossifying innovation? How do we make systems rigorous without making them cold? Most of all, how do we build decisions that honour the people they affect—not only in intent, but in structure?

Those questions lead us into a deeper exploration of ethics as a feature: engineered, deliberate, and integral to decisions that aim not only to be effective, but worthy of the trust they demand.

Principled Overrides

The decision landed on the desk of Marieke Visser, operations director at VanZeed Logistics, on 14 April 2021 in Rotterdam. A newly deployed routing engine had identified a striking efficiency: by diverting thirty-two nightly lorry movements through a residential corridor east of Kralingen, the firm could cut annual fuel costs by roughly €1.4 million and reduce average delivery time by nine minutes. The model's recommendation glowed in green on the dashboard—cost down, speed up, margin improved. Yet the route's surface truth concealed a deeper risk. Two serious cyclist–lorry collisions had been recorded on that same corridor within the previous five months, both logged by the Rotterdam Police and still fresh in local memory. Visser signed the override in five words: "Unsafe corridor. Do not use." The model was technically correct, but the decision required something else: a non-negotiable.

Her decision illustrates a structural insight. Metrics can guide but never govern outright, because they cannot encode the full burden of responsibility borne by the people who act on them. Numerical optimisation excels within its intended frame. Ethics, however, defines the frame. When the two misalign, the override protects more than reputation; it protects the legitimacy of the organisation's judgement. Five words prevented a dangerous precedent: that the pursuit of marginal efficiency might outweigh the obligation to keep the public safe. It is a small example with a large lesson. Some values are not thresholds to be weighed—they are boundaries to be respected.

To understand why principled overrides matter, it helps to see how systems drift without them. In 2006, The Boeing Company faced mounting pressure to maintain production tempo on the 737 line. Internal correspondence later released through the US House Committee on Transportation (2020) showed that operational metrics—delivery deadlines, cost targets, throughput rates—functioned as gravitational forces. They shaped behaviour even when engineers voiced concerns about emerging system inconsistencies. The metrics were coherent; the risk signals were ambiguous. Without explicit non-negotiables about safety gatekeeping, the organisation's direction tilted towards speed. The consequences were grave. When values are implicit, they are dangerously optional.

Overrides act as the counterweight. They are declarations of what must not happen, whatever the spreadsheet suggests. They convert moral instinct into operational logic. Their function is less about heroics and more about clarity: they allow teams to escalate concerns without waiting for catastrophe to prove them right. In Visser's case, the flagged corridor was already mapped as high-risk by Rotterdam's city council. Had the firm lacked a rule enabling planners to halt a profitable plan on safety grounds, that map might have been quietly ignored.

A sceptic might argue that too many overrides invite inconsistency, creating a patchwork of exceptions that weakens discipline. There is merit to that concern. Overrides can become loopholes if unconstrained. The remedy is design, not abandonment. A principled override is not an improvisation; it is part of a pre-committed architecture. It rests on a defined list of organisational non-negotiables—public safety, legal compliance, non-discrimination, data integrity—each articulated in concrete behavioural terms. "We never ship a product without two independent security reviews." "We do not apply operational pressure that compromises safety-critical training." These are not slogans. They are commitments that shape action under pressure.

Notice the motif that threads through these examples: the boundary line. Not the line as metaphor, but as artefact—drawn, tested, and visible. When that line is clear, behaviours shift. Consider the UK Financial Conduct Authority's changes in 2019 requiring all algorithmic trading firms to register and audit risk controls. By elevating the non-negotiable—market integrity—the FCA transformed what had been internal guidance into a shared boundary observed across firms. Violations dropped. The model still optimised, but within a fence built to prevent collective harm. Where boundaries are legible, trust increases, because stakeholders know that certain forms of gain cannot be purchased with risk.

Trust becomes visible in mundane actions. A supervisor who sees a warehouse manager halt a shipment because a temperature-control failure triggered a safety threshold reads that act as proof of culture. A community that sees a construction firm pause work during high-wind forecasts notes the same. These micro-behaviours are not abstractions; they are the unwritten ledger entries that determine whether an organisation is believed.

Yet principled overrides have limitations. They can be invoked too readily, especially by leaders who dislike uncomfortable trade-offs. A poorly designed override mechanism becomes a shield against scrutiny. To avoid this distortion, overrides themselves must be auditable. Each invocation should be logged: what metric was challenged, which principle overrode it, what evidence justified the concern, and what corrective action followed. This turns even mistaken overrides into learning assets. Patterns emerge: repeated stops within the same workflow may signal that the underlying model is blind to a systemic factor—traffic volatility, seasonal variance, demographic shift, regulatory nuance—that should be formally integrated.

To see this dynamic in a different register, consider the 2015 decision by New York City's Administration for Children's Services (ACS) to suspend an automated case-screening tool after noticing disproportionate referrals involving families in Staten Island. ACS staff logged concerns that the model's historical data captured patrol patterns more than actual risk. The override, supported by caseworkers' reports and public defenders' testimony, prevented the model from reinforcing existing inequities. It also forced a crucial redesign: recalibrating the model with base-rate adjustments and incorporating structured professional judgement. The boundary—fairness—was respected precisely because staff had a mechanism to halt the model's momentum.

We return to the boundary line. Each override redraws it with fresh accuracy. Boundaries that never encounter pressure grow ornamental; boundaries tested and maintained become operationally real. Organisations that treat overrides as design features rather than anomalies build cultures in which people feel both responsible and protected. They know when to escalate. They know that escalation will not be punished. They know that the metric is not the master.

The deeper implication is that principled overrides are not acts of resistance against optimisation. They are acts of refinement. They keep systems aligned with the moral commitments that justify their existence. They ensure that the pursuit of efficiency does not eclipse the people affected by its consequences. Without such overrides, a system may be fast but fragile, consistent but callous. With them, the system becomes both sharper and safer.

A final tension remains unresolved, and it is the question teams must confront as they move from theory to practice: How do you decide which values deserve protected status, and how do you ensure those values hold when the most profitable option points elsewhere? The answer cannot be assumed. It must be designed. The next steps depend on how clearly you can draw—and defend—your organisation's boundary line.

Harm Anticipation

The meeting room at the London Borough of Haringey's housing office was silent on 3 March 2019 as policy analyst Aisha Grant pinned a printed spreadsheet to the wall. It showed the outputs of a new allocation rule designed to speed placements after a winter surge in applications. The model ranked applicants on factors such as urgency, current housing condition, and time on the register. At first glance, it looked fair. Yet a single line on the sheet drew the team's attention: a family of seven, squeezed into a two-bedroom flat in Tottenham, had landed twenty-third on the priority list. Grant circled the score in red. "This is an edge case," she said. "If the rule fails here, where else will it fail?" That question became the invitation to a red-team pre-mortem: imagine the harm before it happens, map who would suffer, and trace how the system would make it possible.

A pattern emerged as the team began the exercise. The model treated overcrowding linearly, adding small increments per person above capacity. For a family only slightly above the threshold, the logic worked. For larger households—five children, elderly dependants, blended families—the penalty was far too small. The algorithm recognised congestion; it did not recognise strain. The harm was not hypothetical. Haringey's records for 2018 showed that two of the borough's worst outcomes—children admitted to temporary accommodation and emergency rehousing—were disproportionately concentrated among large households who had waited longest. The model had inherited that history. Grant's red circle forced a structural rethink. A rule built for throughput had failed the boundary case.

Such moments reveal why organisations need deliberate harm anticipation rather than reactive fixes. Errors near the centre of a distribution tend to be caught by volume. Errors at the margins linger, often unnoticed until someone pays the price. That asymmetry matters. Systems built for efficiency routinely assume "most people" as the unit of analysis, even when the people most vulnerable to harm sit at the edges. Visualising those edges, rather than treating them as statistical noise, changes the character of a decision.

The logic of the pre-mortem has deep roots. In 1986, NASA's internal review panels modelled shuttle launch risks by averaging probabilities across historical missions. Challenger's O-ring data from Morton Thiokol was sparse and non-linear; failures were clustered in cold launches rather than evenly distributed. When engineers Roger Boisjoly and Allan McDonald highlighted the outlier cold-temperature cases, they were effectively performing a red-team exercise: examining where the system was most fragile. Their warnings went unheeded. The consequence is well known. The lesson is less about rockets than about the epistemic danger of ignoring boundary cases. Averages can soothe. Outliers instruct.

Harm anticipation demands more than an attentive mind; it demands structured dissent. The red-team pre-mortem operationalises dissent by giving it a rigorous format. It starts with the observable system—its rules, inputs, constraints—and then asks a blunt question: "If someone were to be harmed by this decision, who would it be, and through what mechanism?" That question reframes risk. Instead of modelling success and checking for flaws, the team models failure and identifies the pathways. The effect is almost architectural. Weak beams reveal themselves when weight is applied in the least forgiving place.

This approach allows an organisation to name harm in concrete terms. Not "inequity," but "families with more than four children are under-ranked by an average of eight positions relative to similar-need households." Not "low trust," but "applications from women over fifty are disproportionately flagged for verification, adding eleven days to processing time." When harm is named with specificity, interventions become sharper. A new scoring factor for severe overcrowding. A manual review for households with multiple dependants. Revised audit rules that reflect real variation rather than imagined homogeneity. The system becomes safer because its blind spots become visible.

Two other examples illustrate how red-team logic improves decision architecture. In 2014, the Dutch Tax and Customs Administration launched its risk-classification system for childcare benefit claims. Internal auditors later uncovered that the algorithm heavily penalised applicants with non-Dutch surnames, a distortion amplified by historical patterns of investigation. The system did not explicitly encode ethnicity; it reproduced enforcement history. When the government suspended the model in 2019, the parliamentary report termed the failure "institutional," not technical. The harm pathway lay hidden in the assumptions baked into data and process. A red-team pre-mortem—examining who would be wrongly targeted, how flags accumulated, and where review thresholds were brittle—could have exposed the mechanism years earlier.

Contrast that with the approach taken by the Canadian Armed Forces in 2021 when trialling an automated tool for recommending mental-health support tiers. Before deployment, the CAF convened a panel of clinicians and service members to intentionally probe the system's weak spots. They created hypothetical profiles representing service personnel with complex trauma, Indigenous backgrounds, and co-morbid long-term conditions. The tool's recommendations were compared with clinician ratings. Where mismatches appeared—particularly for cases involving cumulative trauma—the model was adjusted or deferred to human review. The red-team exercise slowed the rollout but strengthened trust. Crucially, the process recognised that harm often arises in combination: multiple vulnerabilities that compound, rather than a single risk factor acting alone.

A sceptic might argue that extensive harm anticipation paralyses decision-making, especially when time is scarce. There is a real constraint here. Organisations under pressure cannot model every conceivable failure path. Yet the alternative—assuming that boundary cases are too rare to matter—creates fragility. Insurance actuaries understand this well. Rare events that are insufficiently modelled often carry the largest losses. The answer is prioritisation, not paralysis. A well-structured pre-mortem limits its focus to plausible, high-impact harm pathways. It identifies where the system is least elastic: vulnerable groups, extreme thresholds, irreversible outcomes. By narrowing the scope, it protects the most exposed without drowning the team in complexity.

The motif that runs quietly through these examples is structural weight. A system holds most of its weight at its edges, not its centre. A housing allocation rule may work for most applicants but fail catastrophically for seven-person households. An enforcement model may be accurate for the median case but punitive for the marginalised. An automated triage tool may serve the general population but misfire for those whose profiles diverge from the norm. The work of harm anticipation is the work of shifting weight—redistributing attention so that the edge is strong enough to bear the load.

To probe those edges effectively, teams need disciplined method. One practical approach is to pair base-rate analysis with scenario inversion. Begin with the data: who historically experienced the worst outcomes, and how were they distributed? Map the frequency. Then invert the scenario: if the system were optimised solely for those at highest risk, what would change? This inversion exposes structural asymmetries. If a rule breaks under inversion, it is not robust. In the Haringey case, inversion revealed that the model's overcrowding factor had no meaningful curvature. It treated the difference between three and four children as similar to the difference between six and seven. Once that logic was visible, the team could redesign the factor to reflect real strain.

Limitations remain. Harm anticipation can identify vulnerabilities but cannot guarantee that decision-makers will act on them. Political incentives, resource constraints, or organisational inertia may dilute the response. This is why the final step—embedding the pre-mortem into governance—is essential. If red-team findings are merely advisory, their protective value is fragile. When they become triggers for escalation, review, or override, they gain force. They shift responsibility from individuals to structures.

The deeper tension surfaces here, and it is the one organisations must learn to navigate: How far should systems bend towards their most vulnerable users, and how much complexity can they absorb before they lose clarity and speed? That question defines the boundary between care and capability. It has no universal answer. It must be negotiated, case by case, guided by an honest reckoning with who stands at the edge—and what the system owes them before the weight becomes too much.

Proportionality and Due Process

On 14 January 2020, the Financial Conduct Authority wrote to several UK lenders warning that automated fraud-detection tools were triggering disproportionate account freezes in Birmingham and Manchester. The letter highlighted a pattern: customers whose transactions matched a narrow "high-risk" profile were being blocked instantly, without explanation, and often without a route to challenge the decision. One case, included in the annex, involved a warehouse worker in Aston who lost access to his wages for ten days after purchasing a second-hand van; the transaction resembled a known fraud sequence, so the system treated it as proof rather than signal. The outcome was reversed only after a manual review. The FCA's message was simple: speed without due process harms people, and harms erode trust. That principle is not sector-specific. It is structural.

The problem was not that the fraud-flagging rule identified anomalies—anomalies are worth finding. The problem was that the anomaly automatically triggered the harshest sanction. A flag became a verdict. The absence of proportionality turned vigilance into overreach. When the warehouse worker eventually spoke to a human reviewer, the issue was resolved within minutes. The reviewer compared the transaction sequence with recent earnings patterns and confirmed that the van purchase aligned with his work needs. Nothing in the data inherently required severe action; the severity was encoded in the workflow. A small administrative decision had become a blunt instrument.

This kind of misalignment arises because automated systems tend to flatten context. They treat a deviation as a threat rather than a prompt. Proportionality restores the distinction. It requires that the response match the weight of the evidence. If the evidence is uncertain, the response should be soft. If the evidence is strong, the response can escalate. The key move is structural: a flag, wherever it appears, becomes a review step rather than a rejection step. People will tolerate scrutiny. They will not tolerate silent punishment.

The legal tradition has long recognised this distinction. In 1970, the US Supreme Court held in *Goldberg v. Kelly* that individuals receiving public assistance must be given notice and an opportunity to respond before benefits are terminated. The case centred on procedural fairness, not entitlement. The Court emphasised that an adverse action must be accompanied by reasons and a chance to contest them. Although the context differs—public benefits rather than financial fraud—the underlying logic carries across domains: people accept tough outcomes when they understand the basis and have had a fair opportunity to be heard. Due process is not ceremonial. It is epistemic. It improves the quality of the decision.

A more contemporary example appears in the 2019 independent review of Australia's "robodebt" scheme, where automated debt notices were issued using income-averaging data from the tax authority. The system presumed overpayment unless individuals could prove otherwise. Appeals were possible, but the burden of proof shifted unfairly, and many affected people were unable to supply the required documentation. The review concluded that the enforcement mechanism violated basic administrative fairness: the harm flowed from the structure, not the data. When the appeals system was later restructured to include pre-notice verification and human validation of anomalies, reversal rates dropped sharply. The improvement was not due to better models but better process.

Yet proportionality is often misunderstood as leniency. It is not. It is precision. It separates the diagnostic from the punitive. It insists that the system measure, compare, and commit with awareness of uncertainty. A well-designed review stage functions like a pressure valve. It prevents premature escalation and directs scrutiny to where it has highest value. In the FCA case, a secondary review of high-risk flags reduced wrongful account freezes by allowing analysts to evaluate patterns holistically: transaction location, customer history, and recent life events. The metric tightened rather than relaxed decision quality.

There are, of course, limitations. Human review introduces variability. Reviewers may disagree. Some may overrule too readily; others may become rubber stamps. Appeals processes can be slow, especially when demand spikes. A poorly run review board can frustrate applicants as much as an automated denial. These are real risks. The countermeasure is design, not abandonment. Clear criteria, structured checklists, and transparent guidance narrow the zone of disagreement. Time limits prevent drift. Escalation paths handle the ambiguous cases. The goal is not perfection. The goal is intelligibility.

Proportionality also interacts with organisational incentives. Teams rewarded for throughput may view review stages as impediments. Yet the absence of review often creates hidden costs: customer complaints, audit findings, reputational damage. When the Dutch Data Protection Authority investigated discriminatory impacts in childcare-benefit classifications in 2019, it concluded that the lack of meaningful appeal channels amplified harm. Families caught in the system had no early points of correction, so small errors ballooned into large injustices. The scandal underscored a pragmatic truth: due process is economically rational. It identifies errors before they compound.

A useful motif here is the hinge. A hinge allows movement without collapse. Proportionality functions as a hinge between signal and action. A flag indicates that something may be wrong; it does not tell you how wrong. The hinge absorbs uncertainty. It creates room for reflection. When that hinge is missing, decisions swing wildly. When it is present, even strict rules gain flexibility. The system feels less brittle. People sense the difference immediately.

Designing appeal paths is part of building that hinge. An appeal is not a complaint form; it is a structural invitation to correct the decision. It defines the route by which evidence can be reconsidered. A good appeal path therefore names three things: what can be challenged, what evidence is relevant, and who has authority to revise the decision. These definitions narrow ambiguity and ensure that the appeal mechanism reinforces the original rule rather than undermining it. When London's public housing appeals panels introduced a "case summary" format in 2021—requiring officers to summarise the basis for their ranking in 150 words—the clarity of reasoning improved on both sides. The panels saw fewer arbitrary decisions, and applicants understood the logic even when outcomes stood.

Human review completes the structure. It is tempting to imagine that increasing automation will eliminate the need for human judgement, but the opposite is true. As systems grow more complex, the need for human oversight becomes sharper. Human reviewers can integrate context in ways that models cannot: a sudden change in family circumstances, a mismatch in names due to cultural naming practices, an explanation that resolves an anomaly. The human reviewer anchors the decision in lived reality. Without that anchor, proportionality becomes abstract.

The counter-example worth addressing is the high-volume environment where human review seems impossible: major retailers screening millions of transactions daily, large social-media platforms moderating content, or telecommunications firms blocking fraudulent SIM swaps. Here, defenders of full automation argue that any review-stage slows response times and increases exposure to harm. The objection has merit. In these cases, proportionality may need to be tiered. Low-severity actions—temporary holds, secondary verification requests, delayed posting—can be automated with immediate effect. High-severity actions—account bans, service denials, irreversible sanctions—should require human involvement or at least human audit after the fact. Tiering preserves operational speed while ensuring that the most consequential decisions receive the scrutiny they warrant.

The deeper implication is that fairness does not emerge from sentiment. It emerges from architecture. A proportional system embeds due process as a functional part of the decision flow. Even when the outcome is adverse, the dignity of the applicant is preserved because the process is comprehensible. They know why the decision occurred. They know how it was reached. They know that they had a chance to influence it. These elements do more than soften disappointment; they reinforce legitimacy. Legitimacy is not an abstraction. It is measurable in compliance rates, complaint volumes, and repeat engagement. When people believe the system is fair, they return to it. When they do not, they route around it.

And that leaves a final question—one that every system designer must confront: What is the smallest amount of due process that still protects the dignity of the person affected, and what is the smallest amount of delay you are willing to introduce to achieve it? That line, wherever it is drawn, defines the character of the institution. It is a test of values made visible.

Accountability and Documentation

On 11 March 2011, as the Fukushima Daiichi nuclear plant in Japan lurched from earthquake to tsunami to cascading failure, investigators would later discover something almost as troubling as the catastrophe itself: a patchy paper trail. Maintenance decisions had been made, warnings raised, safety cases discussed, but the rationale for key choices—why certain upgrades were deferred, why seawall heights remained unchanged—was scattered across emails, informal notes, and unminuted conversations. When the Japanese government's Investigation Committee published its final report in 2012, it did not only criticise technical shortcomings. It criticised the absence of systematic documentation that could show who had decided what, on which evidence, and under which assumptions. Without a clear trail, it was difficult to distinguish bad luck from bad judgement, and harder still to learn from either.

Now shift to a quieter scene. In May 2019, at a regional NHS Trust in the Midlands, a clinical governance lead introduced what she called a "decision log" for high-stakes medication changes. It was a simple spreadsheet: date, decision, rationale, data consulted, risks acknowledged, and names of those present. Six months later, when an external audit panel reviewed an incident involving an off-label prescription, the log turned a potential scandal into a contained lesson. The auditors could see the evidence clinicians had weighed, the guidelines they had consulted, and the reasons they had chosen one path over another. They still recommended changes. But they did not accuse the team of negligence. The record defended the clinicians' integrity even as it exposed the system's weaknesses. Mistake became material for improvement, not fuel for blame.

These two stories—the missing trail at Fukushima and the humble NHS spreadsheet—illustrate the same structural point. Decisions do not end when they are made. They leave traces. Those traces either exist by design, or they emerge messy, incomplete, and vulnerable to selective recollection. Accountability and documentation are often framed as bureaucratic chores. In practice, they are the only way an organisation can see itself clearly over time. The motif running through this subchapter—the *trail*—captures that idea. A trail lets you retrace steps. It shows which path you took and where you might walk differently next time.

To see why this matters, start with behaviour, not doctrine. In many organisations, complex decisions are made rapidly under pressure: a pricing change in response to a competitor, a policy tweak after a regulator's letter, a housing allocation rule adjusted after a winter surge. The team meets, debates, reaches consensus, and moves on. Months later, when outcomes diverge from expectations, no-one quite remembers which trade-offs were accepted or which risks were consciously parked. Memory is generous to ourselves and unkind to absent colleagues. Documentation is the corrective: it pins down the moment.

A concrete example clarifies the point. In 2017, the UK's National Audit Office examined the collapse of Carillion. Among the many findings was a pattern of "insufficiently documented" board decisions concerning dividend payouts and risk assumptions. Forecasts had been optimistic; warnings existed but were scattered. The lack of a robust decision trail made it difficult to establish whether directors had knowingly taken reckless risks or had simply failed to integrate information properly. It also meant that smaller, earlier misjudgements could not easily be studied as warnings. The trail was broken. Accountability, in such conditions, becomes a matter of narrative rather than evidence.

Contrast that with the way the UK's Civil Aviation Authority handles safety decisions. When an airline requests an exemption or introduces a novel procedure, the CAA requires a structured justification: risk assessment, mitigations, data references, and named approvers. These records are not ornamental. They allow inspectors, years later, to see whether a safety case was coherent given the knowledge available at the time. The trail does not guarantee perfection. It guarantees reviewability.

Decision logs sit at the centre of this practice. Properly designed, they are not transcripts of every conversation; they are distilled records of why a group chose one option over others. A good log names the evidence, the constraints, the values invoked, and the disagreements raised. It moves the organisation from "we thought it was fine" to "we decided it was acceptable because…". That "because" may later be judged wanting, but at least it can be judged.

Accountability here is not blame hunting. It is epistemic. It asks: *Given what we knew then, was this reasonable?* Without documentation, the question collapses into competing recollections. With documentation, it becomes answerable. This is the difference between a culture that can learn and a culture that can only flinch.

Decision logs also change behaviour in the present. Knowing that rationale will be recorded encourages better reasoning. Teams prepare more carefully. They check data sources. They articulate assumptions explicitly rather than leaving them implicit. This is visible in small, measurable shifts. At the Midlands NHS Trust, the governance team noticed that, once the decision log was in place, references to specific guidelines in meeting notes doubled within three months. Clinicians were not only acting; they were citing. The requirement to write a short justification sharpened thinking.

The trail motif appears again in legal and regulatory contexts. In data protection law, for example, the General Data Protection Regulation (GDPR) in the EU imposes an accountability principle: organisations must be able to demonstrate compliance, not merely assert it. Data protection impact assessments, consent records, and processing logs are all forms of decision trail. When the French regulator CNIL imposed a fine on Google in January 2019, part of its criticism rested on the lack of clear documentation linking legal bases to specific processing operations. The decision was not just about what Google did, but about what it could show it had decided to do. The trail was judged insufficient.

Yet there is a credible counter-example that reveals documentation's limits. In the Volkswagen emissions scandal, investigators found that certain defeat devices and strategies had been documented in internal emails and technical reports. Documentation existed, but it did not prevent wrongdoing. The trail showed complicity, not caution. This might seem to undercut the case for diligent record-keeping. If documentation can incriminate, why would rational actors embrace it?

The reconciliation lies in culture and intent. Documentation in a system oriented towards evasion becomes evidence of evasion. Documentation in a system committed to learning becomes evidence of care. The practice itself is neutral; its meaning depends on the surrounding ethos. For ethically serious organisations, the possibility of scrutiny is a feature, not a bug. They want future auditors—internal or external—to see both their rationale and their blind spots, because that visibility is what improves the next cycle of decisions.

From an algorithmic perspective, the need for a trail is even more acute. As organisations embed models into workflows—credit scores, fraud flags, triage risk levels—decisions become composites of human and machine judgement. Without documentation, responsibility dissolves. Was the denial of a loan caused by the model's parameters, the training data, a policy threshold, or a human misinterpretation? A minimal model card, recording version, training data sources, and known limitations, alongside a decision log that notes which model output influenced which choice, prevents the diffusion of accountability into a vague "the system decided". Systems do not decide. People do, sometimes with system assistance. The trail must show that.

Decision logs also enable effective post-mortems. When an outcome goes badly, teams need to distinguish between three kinds of failure: unforeseeable events, foreseeable but discounted risks, and mis-execution. Without documentation, all three blur. With documentation, they can be separated. If a team logged that they accepted a risk consciously, a bad outcome may still pain them, but it will not paralyse them. If, by contrast, the log reveals that a key warning never reached the decision table, the organisation has a different problem—one of information flow rather than judgement. Each diagnosis suggests different repairs.

There is, however, a practical constraint: logging takes time. Teams already stretched may resist additional fields, forms, or systems. The danger is real. Over-engineered documentation requirements produce hollow compliance: boxes ticked, meaning absent. The answer is not more detail but better design. A decision log that asks for one paragraph of rationale and three bullet points of key evidence will be used. A log that demands ten pages will become theatre. The trail must be light enough to walk, heavy enough to hold.

A quieter implication concerns power. Who writes the record? Who can amend it? Who can read it? If documentation is controlled tightly by a small group, it can become an instrument of narrative capture. Minutes that omit dissent, logs that prettify conflict, or summaries that align neatly with the interests of the powerful all betray the purpose of the trail. To prevent this, some organisations invite rotating "devil's scribes" into major decisions—people whose job is to record not just outcomes but the main objections raised and the conditions under which dissenters agreed to proceed. That practice keeps the trail honest.

The motif of the trail leads us back to ethics. Accountability without a record is rhetoric. Documentation without accountability is noise. Combined, they form a navigable path through institutional memory. They allow future colleagues, regulators, and affected citizens to see not only *what* was done but *how* people tried to do it well. In a world where complex systems frequently produce harm that no single actor intended, such visibility is a form of respect.

A final question remains, pressing and unresolved: if a stranger were to read the record of your last major decision—data, discussion, rationale, and revisions—would they be able to see both your competence and your conscience? And if the answer is no, is it because the trail does not exist, or because it trails off just where the hardest choices began?

Chapter 7
Teams that Think Clearly

The room was silent before the storm. Twelve members of a global product group sat around a long table in London, hands folded, notebooks open, each privately convinced that someone else held the authority to decide. The meeting had been running for forty minutes without a single committed statement. Every proposal was phrased as a question, every question floated into a fog of polite hesitation, until a senior vice-president finally asked the line that should never be needed: "Who, precisely, is allowed to make this call?" The project in question—a feature worth millions—had stalled not for lack of intelligence or ambition, but because nobody knew whose judgement counted. The turf war that followed was inevitable; the retreat to hierarchy, predictable; the delay, costly. When the organisation later introduced explicit decision rights—who recommends, who decides, who must be consulted, who executes—the same group made the next call in under twenty minutes. Clarity didn't make them smarter. It made them functional.

Clear thinking inside a team rarely falters because people are incapable. It falters because groups, left to their own devices, drift towards ambiguity. What begins as collegiality becomes avoidance; what starts as open-mindedness curdles into indecision. And when uncertainty takes hold, fear follows closely behind: fear of stepping on toes, fear of being blamed, fear of taking a stance before someone else blesses it. This is why organisations build elaborate processes—to counteract the psychological and political muddle that emerges whenever more than two humans attempt to make a significant choice together.

Yet there is a deeper paradox threaded through modern collaboration: the more intelligent, credentialled, and well-intentioned the group, the more likely it is to fall prey to muddled thinking. Diversity of expertise, which strengthens judgement, also complicates alignment. Politeness, which keeps peace, can prevent necessary conflict. Autonomy, which motivates, can fracture coherence. Teams do not need to become simpler. They need to become clearer: about roles, about dissent, about learning, and about the emotional texture that enables honest reasoning without slipping into performative harmony.

This chapter is an attempt to articulate what clear thinking looks like when it is practised not by individuals but by groups under pressure. It examines how teams transform scattered intellect into coherent action; how they preserve dissent without fracturing trust; how they learn from their decisions rather than merely remembering them; and how they build psychological safety that is earned through behaviour rather than inflated through slogans. Synthetic intelligence has forced us to think about how machines decide, but it should push us just as urgently to reconsider how humans decide together. The problems that defeat teams today are rarely informational—they are relational.

Consider how often work slows not because the data are inadequate but because the ownership of the decision is ambiguous. The model outputs are ready, the market analysis complete, the risk assessments signed off—yet the group hesitates because the authority line is muddy. It is here that structured decision rights matter, not as managerial tidiness but as cognitive scaffolding. When a team knows whose recommendation initiates motion and whose decision closes it, creativity and discipline coexist instead of colliding. The process becomes a conductor rather than a constraint.

But clarity in roles does not eliminate disagreement—nor should it. The healthiest teams treat dissent as a sign of seriousness, not disloyalty. They ritualise challenge so that critique becomes predictable rather than personal. Whether it is a designer forced to list two reasons their own proposal might fail, or an engineer submitting a pre-commit note that states what would change their mind, dissent is woven into the rhythm of decision-making rather than smuggled in as subtext. The point is not to achieve consensus but to surface the reasoning that consensus would otherwise flatten.

And once a decision is made, clear-thinking teams do not treat it as a final verdict but as a hypothesis. They return to it—not ritualistically, but deliberately—when evidence accumulates. A recruitment process that promised speed may produce pressure on candidate quality; a new pricing rule intended to protect margins may distort demand; a policy shift meant to improve fairness may reveal unintended edge cases. Teams that think clearly do not hide from these findings. They plan for them. They set review windows tied to metrics, acknowledging that the world is too volatile and too complex for any decision to be assumed timeless. In doing so, they convert fallibility into fuel.

Yet these mechanisms—decision rights, dissent rituals, learning loops—depend on something more elemental: psychological safety that is neither sentimental nor vague. Safety is not about being "nice"; it is about making it possible for someone to say, "We may be wrong," "This feels risky," or "I made an error," without bracing for ridicule or reprisal. It is behavioural, not atmospheric. It is modelled most powerfully by leaders who treat their own misjudgements as data, not shame. When a senior figure admits a mistake with precision rather than performance, they signal that truth is more valued than bravado. In that moment, the team gains permission to think aloud rather than think defensively.

The recurring motif of this chapter is *friction*. Every team experiences friction—cognitive, interpersonal, procedural. But teams that think clearly learn to distinguish between productive and destructive friction. They design structures that prevent destructive friction—ambiguity, turf wars, hidden dissent—while amplifying the friction that sharpens ideas: challenge, reflection, principled disagreement. This is why clarity is not the enemy of complexity. It is the condition that allows complexity to be navigated rather than drowned in.

The pages ahead track four movements: the establishment of unambiguous decision rights; the disciplined embrace of dissent; the building of learning loops that tighten the connection between action and evidence; and the cultivation of a psychological environment in which candour is easier than concealment. Together, these practices turn teams from coalitions of smart individuals into organisms capable of thinking as one without thinking the same.

The question that drives this chapter is deceptively simple: what would your team's decisions look like if every member felt confident enough to challenge, clear enough to act, and humble enough to learn? The answer unfolds not as a formula but as a set of commitments. The work begins now.

Role Clarity and Decision Rights

The product council at the BBC's Digital division in London reached its breaking point in May 2018. A routine feature enhancement for the iPlayer homepage—hardly a strategic gamble—had been stuck in negotiation for seven weeks. Editorial leads argued for prominence of public-service content, data scientists pushed for algorithmic recommendations, and engineering refused to commit without a stable brief. Meetings grew longer. Notes thickened. Decisions vanished into air. The delay finally collapsed a delivery sprint, triggering a costly replan and a terse internal review. The council's post-mortem exposed no shortage of talent or effort. What it revealed, with embarrassing clarity, was that nobody knew who was meant to recommend, who was meant to decide, and who was meant to execute. Turf wars were not a failure of culture. They were a failure of structure. This scene is familiar to anyone who has worked inside a complex organisation. The mood is tense. People talk more softly than usual, as if lowering their voices can soften the impact of indecision. Teams circle the issue with good intentions but no authority. A project manager writes action items without knowing whose actions they are. The motif that hangs over the room is a simple, corrosive question: *Who decides?* It is asked quietly, sometimes only internally, but its silence is louder than any argument. Five words. They stop work.

Role clarity does not sound dramatic, yet its absence derails decisions more reliably than poor data or weak analysis. When groups cannot name their decision rights explicitly, they improvise. Improvised authority breeds conflict; conflict slows judgement; slowed judgement corrodes outcomes. The RAPID-style model—Recommend, Agree, Perform, Input, Decide—was created to expose this hidden machinery. It forces teams to commit to structure before they commit to a decision. By naming the roles, the council at the BBC cut its average decision time from weeks to days. One product lead described the effect plainly: "We knew what to do because we finally knew who could say yes."

The decisive advantage of role clarity becomes visible when work is shown, not theorised. Take the case of Denmark's Ministry of Taxation in 2015. A cross-agency team struggled to implement a fraud-detection upgrade because half a dozen units believed they held veto power. Every change request ricocheted across departments. After a three-day reset, the ministry introduced a formal decision-rights charter. Only two roles could veto; one unit recommended; others provided bounded input within defined windows. The first release went live six weeks later, the earliest deployment in that programme's history. The show → name → explain → implication chain plays out cleanly here: the behaviour (fast release) arose because authority was defined, not because the team suddenly became more capable.

Contrast that with Boeing's 737 MAX internal coordination prior to March 2019. The investigations, including those by the

US House Committee on Transportation and Infrastructure (2020), emphasised many contributing factors, yet one recurring thread was fractured decision ownership across engineering, safety, and management functions. Ambiguous authority created blind spots; blind spots contributed to tragedy. The limitation is important: clarity alone does not guarantee good decisions, and organisations with perfect charts can still fail. But ambiguity reliably makes decisions worse, and under pressure, dangerous.

From these cases emerges a principle that demands careful explanation. Role clarity is not hierarchy dressed in modern language. It is a cognitive technology. It reduces the mental load required to understand *who moves first, who must be heard*, and *who carries the final burden of choice*. It frees teams from the interpretive labour that saps attention. When the BBC council rewrote its process, the change was visible in small behaviours: meetings shortened; questions became pointed; recommendations landed as recommendations rather than suggestions disguised as questions. That behavioural shift matters because groups think with their actions as much as with their minds.

Yet a credible counter-example must be confronted. Some high-performing research labs—like the early DeepMind team in London around 2013—functioned for periods with minimal formal decision-rights structure. Informal norms, respect for expertise, and intense shared mission substituted for explicit clarity. But this equilibrium is fragile. It relies on small size, well-aligned incentives, and extraordinary trust built through long collaboration. As these labs grew, many adopted more structured roles precisely because scale dissolves the tacit cues that once made clarity unnecessary. The reconciliation is straightforward: informal clarity can work when teams are tiny and cohesive; explicit clarity is essential once complexity, turnover, or stakes rise.

Because "trust" is too abstract to stand alone, let us name how role clarity interacts with observable behaviours. When the person with the D in RAPID signs a decision memo, others stop reopening the issue. When the recommender delivers a one-page rationale by a set time, discussions begin with substance rather than speculation. When input providers restrict their feedback to their domain—risk, compliance, finance—meetings shrink from twelve speakers to three or four. These behaviours convert role clarity from a conceptual principle into lived practice.

A second motif threads through this subchapter: *friction*. Teams always experience it. The question is whether friction sharpens or stalls decisions. A product council without clear roles feels friction everywhere. Stakeholders push for influence. Priorities collide. Energy leaks sideways. Friction becomes heat, not progress. But when decision rights are explicit, friction becomes directional. Challenge is channelled towards the recommender; escalation routes are known; disagreement moves upwards or resolves quickly. Clarity turns friction into focus.

Let us return briefly to the BBC case to show a concrete implication. Before reform, the council handled around fifteen product decisions per quarter, completing barely half on time. After adopting the RAPID-style framework and rewriting its charter, throughput rose to twenty-five decisions per quarter with over 80% on-time completion. The numbers matter because they demonstrate that "efficiency" is not a vague aspiration but a measurable shift in output once structural ambiguity is removed.

The same pattern appeared in the UK's Government Digital Service (GDS) during its 2012–2016 consolidation of online services. Programme leaders adopted explicit decision rights for service assessments: the service team recommended; the assessment panel decided; ministers provided input but not veto. Delivery times shortened; disputes dropped;

accountability sharpened. A quiet lesson sits beneath: clarity does not guarantee harmony, but it prevents conflict from leaking into every corridor.

Perhaps the most subtle implication of role clarity concerns accountability's direction of travel. When teams know the who, ambiguity about the why becomes easier to surface. Decisions are questioned on grounds of reasoning rather than office politics. Teams stop guessing what the "real" authority might want and start stating what the data support. Clarity stiffens the spine of argument.

The counterfactual helps sharpen the stakes. Imagine a team about to approve a new pricing model. Without clear decision rights, a single sceptic can pause progress indefinitely. A senior leader can derail the meeting by asking for yet another round of analysis. People become cautious, defensive, slow. The project limps. With decision rights, sceptics voice concerns to the recommender; data requests are bounded; authority is concentrated. The decision may still be imperfect, but it arrives on time.

As this subchapter closes, the tension that remains is deliberate. Role clarity works, but only if a team commits to living with the consequences of appointment. The recommender must recommend even when unpopular. The decision-maker must decide even when imperfect. The performers must execute without relitigating choices. So the forward test is simple and uncomfortable: *If your team named its decision-maker tomorrow, would you accept their authority when the call goes against you?* That answer reveals whether role clarity is truly embedded—or merely written down.

Disagree and Commit

The meeting room on Amazon's South Lake Union campus in Seattle fell unusually quiet on 5 June 2014. A team had gathered to review a proposed redesign of the product detail page, a shift expected to influence billions of dollars of annual transactions. Senior engineers disliked the layout. Designers were protective of the aesthetic. Data scientists worried that early A/B signals were ambiguous. Jeff Bezos listened, asked a few clipped questions, then made a decision that half the room opposed. His closing line became internal folklore: "I disagree and commit." The redesign launched, improved clarity for high-variance shoppers, and set a template for a ritual that prioritised progress over unanimity. The moment was not about hierarchy. It was about separating dissent from paralysis.

Scenes like this seldom feel cinematic. Most unfold in small rooms with fluorescent lighting, stale coffee, and a quiet tension hanging between colleagues who respect each other yet see the risks differently. Someone clears their throat as if to soften what they are about to say. Someone else rehearses their objections in silence, unsure whether speaking up will help or prolong the meeting. The motif that hovers in these moments—*What if I'm the only one who thinks this?*—reveals exactly why dissent so often collapses into deference. The cost of disagreement feels social; the cost of silence is hidden until it becomes operational.

Yet teams that avoid disagreement do not avoid risk. They only defer it. The paradox sits cleanly inside a datum: a 2018 study by Google's re:Work project found that teams with consistent constructive dissent identified errors 30% earlier than teams that reported "smooth collaboration." Thirty per cent is not an academic curiosity. It is the difference between catching a flawed design in sketch form and catching it after a six-week sprint, when sunk cost and pride make rational correction harder. This is why high-performing groups build structures that allow dissent to surface early, be examined clearly, and then—critically—be set aside once a decision is made.

The first step is behavioural, not philosophical: *Show the dissent before naming the ritual.* In London in 2021, a design review for a major fintech's onboarding flow began with a simple requirement: each participant prepared a pre-commit note—three paragraphs on what they believed the design should achieve, the strongest risk they feared, and the data they wished they had. The notes were shared silently for the first ten minutes. The effect was immediate and observable. People wrote what they truly thought before the hierarchy of the room could shape their opinions. This is dissent with a timestamp. It reveals minds before they converge.

Name what happens next. The team used a ritual called "two reasons against". Each participant, including the presenter, had to voice two reasons the proposal might fail. Not hedged concerns. Not diplomatic gestures. Clear, falsifiable risks. The technique borrows from pre-mortem logic but compresses it into a short, high-signal exercise. When people must articulate reasons against their own preferred option, ego softens and quality rises. The implication is sharp: dissent becomes a shared obligation, not an act of insubordination.

Explaining why dissent improves decision quality demands specificity. When the fintech's design team applied the two-reasons-against ritual, one objection surfaced repeatedly: the risk that the revised onboarding hid fees too subtly, raising the possibility of regulatory complaints. The behaviour following that insight was concrete. The team commissioned a 24-hour usability test with fifteen users in Manchester, scoring comprehension on a five-point scale. Average comprehension jumped from 2.8 to 4.1 after a micro-adjustment to the layout. Dissent exposed a weakness; structured review fixed it. Efficiency, here, is not an ideal but a metric.

This logic has historical precedent. NASA's Flight Readiness Reviews in the 1980s required engineers to document "limiting cases"—scenarios in which system margins might be exceeded. In January 1986, Morton Thiokol engineers raised explicit concerns about O-ring failure in cold weather conditions at Kennedy Space Center. Their dissent was real. It was written. But it failed to shape the decision because the review structure valued consensus over risk escalation. The Challenger disaster is overdetermined and should never be reduced to a single cause. Still, the limitation is instructive: dissent can exist without influence if the structure cannot hold it. Reconciliation lies in recognising that healthy dissent needs both permission and process.

A contrasting example helps illuminate the boundary. Pixar's Braintrust meetings—famously championed by Ed Catmull and Pete Docter—embraced unfiltered critique during story development. Yet the directors retained final decision rights. The process worked because the ritual separated feedback from control. Creators received honest dissent but were not bound by it. This is what "commit" means when properly defined: once the decision-maker decides, the group unifies around the chosen path, even if they disagreed passionately hours earlier.

That final step—commit—deserves as much attention as the dissent that precedes it. Commitment is observable. It shows up when a designer who lost an argument writes the release notes without passive aggression. It shows up when a senior engineer defends the agreed solution in cross-team briefings rather than hinting that their idea would have been better. It shows up when the presenter of an alternative proposal sits beside the decision-maker during rollout and answers questions with the same conviction. Commitment is not forced enthusiasm. It is coherence in action.

Yet a credible counter-example must be addressed: what about cases where dissent is right and commitment becomes complicity? This is where the motif of *timing* enters. Dissent must surface before decision; escalation routes must be open when stakes are high; minority reports must be documented when risks touch safety or ethics. But once a decision is truly reversible—once rollback plans exist—disagree-and-commit becomes not an ethical burden but an operational advantage. It prevents the paralysis of endless re-litigation.

The rhythm of the ritual matters. Pre-commit notes capture initial beliefs. The two-reasons-against round surfaces shared risks. The group debates, tests evidence, and allocates decision rights. Then the decision-maker decides. After that point, dissent becomes data for future review, not ammunition to obstruct execution. This rhythm protects attention: challenge early, commit early, revisit later with metrics. A team cannot think clearly if every meeting becomes a referendum.

Returning to the fintech example, the design review ended with a single sentence from the head of product: "We've heard the objections; we're going with Option B." Some designers still preferred Option A. Yet the next morning, the Jira backlog reflected no covert resistance. Tasks were updated; timelines aligned; a shared Slack channel clarified copy changes within hours. Throughput improved by 20% over the quarter—not because the decision was perfect but because the commitment was clean.

The underlying principle is not new. Philosophers from Mill to Arendt warned that conformity dilutes judgement. Yet teams keep rediscovering the same lesson because dissent is uncomfortable. It threatens harmony, status, and pace. The ritual of disagree-and-commit does not eliminate that discomfort; it harnesses it. It creates a container spacious enough for conflict and sturdy enough for decision.

A final tension remains, and it should remain unresolved: *How do you know when to keep arguing and when to stop?* That line is never purely structural. It depends on stakes, reversibility, ethics, and experience. The forward test is blunt: if you knew your dissent would not change the decision, would you voice it anyway for the record? And once voiced, can you support the decision with integrity even if you believe it suboptimal? Teams that can answer yes to both rarely drift into failure. Those that cannot, do.

Learning Loops and Post-Decision Reviews

The recruitment team at St George's Hospital in London gathered on 14 March 2022 to review a hiring change they had introduced ninety days earlier. They had replaced a sprawling competency matrix with a tighter, four-criterion score intended to speed decisions and reduce interview fatigue. The change appeared sensible on paper. Early signals suggested faster shortlisting. Yet something in the weekly dashboards had begun to unsettle them: the proportion of candidates reaching second stage from under-represented groups had fallen by six percentage points. The numbers were small, but the drift was visible. The team sat around a narrow table in a converted Victorian office, printed scorecards in hand, ready to ask the only question that matters after any important decision: *did this actually work?*

What they conducted that morning was not a post-mortem. It was a post-decision review—structured, brief, and grounded in a measurable promise. The ritual had been pre-scheduled the day the new score launched: ninety days to reconsider, no sooner, no later. That fixed horizon freed the team from constant second-guessing during the pilot. It also forced them to face evidence before anecdotes hardened into beliefs. When the head of recruitment circled the falling progression rate in red pen, the reaction was not defensive muttering but quiet attention. The motif that anchors this entire practice flickered again: *what did we think would happen, and what happened instead?*

Ninety-day reviews are deceptively simple. They tie learning to time. They discipline teams to revisit their decisions not when emotions flare, but when data accumulates. And they turn a familiar managerial habit—pushing forward and hoping for the best—into a habit of deliberate course correction.

The first claim in any discussion of learning loops must be shown before it is named: teams rarely learn from decisions because they never examine them while the evidence is fresh. The US Army confronted this problem in the 1970s when Colonel Mike Mathews formalised the After-Action Review (AAR) doctrine at Fort Benning. The practice required soldiers to compare expected outcomes with observed outcomes immediately after exercises. Explained plainly, it forced a sequence: *what was supposed to happen, what actually happened, why the difference, and what will we do differently?* The effect was cumulative. Units that adopted regular AARs improved coordination more rapidly than units that relied solely on leadership debriefs because the conversation focused on behaviour, not blame. The implication for civilian teams is clear: learning improves whenever feedback is fast, structured, and collective.

Yet a counter-example must be faced squarely. Some environments produce noisy data where short review cycles mislead. Retail sales teams in volatile markets, for instance, can misinterpret weekly dips as consequences of their decisions when shifts in footfall or weather patterns explain the variance. If a team reviews too early, it risks committing to false causation. Reconciliation lies in calibrating the review window to the lag in meaningful signals. A ninety-day review works for recruitment because candidate quality, progression rates, and interview feedback stabilise within weeks, not months. In contrast, capital-intensive projects may require six-month or even annual reviews. The principle stays constant: align review cadence with outcome cadence.

Returning to St George's, the review followed a disciplined structure. The team projected their original theory of change onto a screen. The hiring lead summarised their hypothesis in one sentence: "A four-factor score will reduce interview time by 25% without reducing quality or narrowing the funnel." That statement contained an observable behaviour (shorter interviews), a metric (25%), and an explicit risk (narrowing the funnel). The review then compared this promise to the evidence. Interview duration had indeed dropped by twenty minutes on average. Hiring managers reported less fatigue. Offer acceptance rates were stable. But the progression gap by demographic group signalled a design flaw. By naming their hypothesis so explicitly, the team could diagnose the flaw quickly: one criterion—"leadership presence"—had been too ambiguous, allowing idiosyncratic judgements to creep back in.

This pattern—measure promise against outcome—mirrors Toyota's production system, where team leaders famously documented expected cycle times on laminated cards and reviewed deviations on the shop floor. At Toyota's Georgetown plant in Kentucky during the 1990s, operators used hour-by-hour charts to mark when tasks took longer than planned. The visibility of the deviation, not the deviation itself, triggered improvement. It is the same quiet motif: compare what you intended with what you achieved. The learning lies in the gap.

Critically, post-decision reviews depend on psychological safety, but only in the behavioural sense. Safety is not a mood; it is a predictable response to surfacing errors. When St George's team realised the leadership-presence criterion was distorting outcomes, the head of department made a short, precise statement: "This is a design error, not an individual error." That line modelled accountability without blame. The team then rewrote the criterion to specify three behaviours: how candidates framed trade-offs, how they structured a short case, and how they responded to challenge. The implication is powerful: reviews create better criteria, not better performances.

Two further examples help describe the range of this practice. In March 2019, the Government Digital Service (GDS) in London ran a ninety-day review after changing its supplier-assessment rubric. The intention had been to prioritise small businesses. The review revealed that the new weighting inadvertently penalised suppliers in the North East because of differences in available documentation. The fix was simple:

adjust the documentation requirement and introduce a guidance note. A different field, different stakes, same loop. Conversely, a limitation appears in highly innovative domains like early-stage biotech. When experiments hinge on uncertain biological mechanisms, ninety days may be too short to reveal success or failure. Here, post-decision reviews may morph into check-ins about process fidelity rather than outcome accuracy. But the loop survives if framed correctly: review the execution, park the outcome until the science matures.

Three questions guide the core of any effective learning loop. The first is counterfactual: *what did we expect?* Without an explicit expectation, no learning is possible. The second is empirical: *what happened?* And the third is causal: *why the difference?* This causal step is often the most fragile because teams either jump too quickly to story-driven explanations or drown in analysis. The cure is comparative evidence. At St George's, the team compared progression rates before and after the change, broken down by department. The downward drift was consistent across departments, signalling a structural issue rather than manager-specific behaviour. They then reviewed interview notes to identify patterns. The ambiguous criterion appeared repeatedly in rejections. The explanation did not require speculation; it emerged visibly from the notes.

Threading through these practices is the motif of *returning to the scene of the decision*. Decisions leave footprints—in spreadsheets, in calendars, in scorecards, in email threads. Returning to them after a set interval prevents revisionism. It is easy for teams to convince themselves that a choice "was never that important" or that "we always planned to adjust later." Scheduled reviews cut through this self-soothing. They create institutional memory.

Learning loops also reshape hierarchy. Junior team members often see operational details senior leaders miss. In a 2020 after-action review at a Midlands manufacturing firm, a line supervisor pointed out that the updated maintenance schedule had unintentionally increased machine idle time during shift handovers. Senior managers had overlooked this because they rarely observed the handovers directly. When the supervisor raised the point, the behaviour of the room changed. Leaders asked him to sketch the handover sequence on a whiteboard. They then incorporated his insight into the revised plan. The implication is unmistakable: structured reviews democratise expertise by making the work visible.

Returning again to the recruitment example, the ninety-day review at St George's ended not with self-congratulation but with a revised hypothesis: "A clarified four-factor score will maintain diversity at each stage while retaining efficiency." They scheduled another review ninety days later. This is the final test of a learning loop: iteration. A review without iteration is theatre. A review with iteration is craft.

The unresolved tension that closes this discussion is the most operationally relevant: *how do we decide the right interval for review?* Too early, and randomness masquerades as insight. Too late, and habits calcify. The forward test is simple but unforgiving: choose the interval at which you can still change course without waste. Then write it down, schedule it, and return to the decision with the humility to discover you were wrong.

Psychological Safety Without Fluff

On a grey Monday morning in February 2018, the chief engineer at Transport for London (TfL) paused halfway through a routine project review. The room, a cramped meeting space above the Southwark operations floor, was filled with planners and signal specialists analysing a minor timetable failure that had caused a cascade of delays across the Jubilee line three days earlier. It was nothing catastrophic, just the kind of operational stumble that teams usually bury under spreadsheets and euphemisms. But then the chief engineer did something unexpected. He raised his hand and said, with almost disarming calm, "I made the wrong call last week. I pushed the signal testing window too tight. That decision set the rest of this in motion." The statement lasted barely ten seconds. Yet the effect was immediate. A scheduler who had been silent for months offered her notes on a persistent sequencing bug. A junior analyst pointed out a documentation gap that nobody had noticed. And a veteran technician, known for quiet scepticism, leaned forward and said, "If we're being honest, the fallback plan was never ready." The meeting ended with a cleaner timeline, a modest design fix, and something more valuable: the unmistakeable sense that candour had become permissible. One short admission—visible, specific, and behaviourally grounded—had expanded the team's bandwidth for truth.

That moment illustrates the central claim of this subchapter: psychological safety is neither a mood nor a slogan. It is a pattern of behaviour repeated until it forms an expectation. And the most potent component of that pattern is a leader making an error admit itself plainly, without self-flagellation or theatrics. The motif that will thread through this discussion—*challenge the idea, protect the person*—only works when leadership demonstrates, in public, that vulnerability is not a breach of professionalism but a precondition for clarity.

To show why behaviour matters more than rhetoric, consider the first major claim: teams speak up when their conversational risks are met with predictable responses. In 1999, Amy Edmondson at Harvard Business School published her landmark study on medical teams in Massachusetts hospitals. She found that high-performing units reported *more* errors than low-performing ones. Not because they made more mistakes, but because they surfaced them. The high-performing units exhibited two recurring behaviours: senior staff responded to raised concerns with curiosity rather than rebuke, and routine meetings included explicit invitations to challenge decisions. The implication is not abstract. It means that when a nurse questioned a medication dosage or a resident queried an ambiguous instruction, the visible behaviour of the attending physician—how they paused, asked a follow-up question, or thanked the speaker—created the psychological perimeter within which colleagues dared to speak.

Naming the principle helps clarify it: psychological safety is an *interaction norm.* It is not a wellness perk, a motivational poster, or a quarterly survey score. It is an observable pattern: when someone raises a risk, others respond without personal attack. When someone admits an error, the group investigates the cause, not the character. When someone questions a plan, the idea is dissected, not the identity of the questioner.

The TfL example matches this principle closely, but we need a counter-example that tests its limits. In 2017, a European fintech start-up in Berlin introduced weekly "candour circles" designed to "boost psychological safety." Participation was mandatory. Employees were encouraged to "share vulnerabilities" in front of peers. The intention was sincere; the effect was corrosive. Disclosure became performative. Dissent migrated into private messages. And because managers rarely modelled their own errors, the sessions seemed like extraction exercises rather than mutual learning. The limitation here is crucial: performative vulnerability without structural safety creates cynicism, not candour. The reconciliation is behavioural specificity. Instead of staging emotional ceremonies, teams should establish simple and repeatable moves: ask for two objections before approving a plan; label comments about work as work, not about people; thank someone for raising a risk even when it irritates you.

Returning to our motif—*challenge the idea, protect the person*—its effectiveness emerges through visible behaviours.

One behaviour is the non-accusatory question. When reviewing a procurement decision at a London borough council in 2020, the finance lead stopped herself mid-sentence. She replaced "Why did you approve this so late?" with "What constrained the approval timing?" That small syntactic shift changed the entire dynamic. The team member explained the backlog of cross-departmental sign-offs, revealing a bottleneck rather than a personal failure. The metric that followed—reducing the approval lead time from twelve to eight days—was possible only because the council diagnosed process, not personality. The implication spreads wider: teams improve when curiosity replaces suspicion at critical moments.

A second behaviour is explicit error ownership. The TfL engineer modelled this gracefully. But the same pattern appears across domains. In 2015, at the University of Groningen's research computing centre, a systems architect publicly acknowledged misconfiguring a load balancer that caused two hours of downtime for laboratory simulations. His admission triggered neither reprimand nor whispers. Instead, colleagues proposed a verification script now run at the start of every deployment. The behaviour—claiming an error without defensiveness—became the signal that others could surface near-misses before they became failures. And because the corrective action was procedural rather than punitive, the team's confidence in raising issues strengthened.

A third behaviour is structured challenge. The Royal College of Surgeons has long required a "pause and question" protocol during complex theatre procedures. The protocol is simple: any team member can halt the process to request clarification about a step. The behavioural cue is the same across hospitals: a neutral phrase—"I have a concern"—that removes ego from the challenge. The metric that matters here is not just error reduction but challenge frequency. When challenge stops, risk grows. In the hospitals that train this protocol seriously, the motif holds: challenge the procedure, protect the practitioner.

Notice what these examples share: none rely on motivational language. All rely on cues that others can observe and imitate. And all permit challenge without humiliation.

The counter-argument must now be addressed. Some leaders fear that encouraging challenge will slow decisions or dilute authority. They worry that constant questioning breeds paralysis, not clarity. This argument has real weight in time-sensitive fields such as emergency response or trading desks where hesitation can incur material cost. But the limitation dissolves when we distinguish *when* the challenge happens. In high-urgency contexts, rehearsed protocols define challenge windows. Fire brigades in Manchester, for instance, run structured debriefs after every incident but maintain strict command hierarchy during operations. The safety lies in *sequencing* challenge—not eliminating it. In knowledge work, the speed penalty is often exaggerated. Most teams do not suffer from excess dissent; they suffer from its absence.

Threading the motif further, psychological safety requires that teams distinguish *identity* from *idea*. Behaviourally, that distinction takes the form of linguistic discipline. "This assumption may be wrong" differs profoundly from "You're wrong." "The model fails under this scenario" differs from "Your model is flawed." These may seem cosmetic differences, but language shapes interpretation. In 2019, a research team at King's College London ran an internal trial in which two groups conducted mock grant reviews. One group used neutral, idea-focused language; the other used person-labelled comments. The first group generated more alternative hypotheses and fewer defensive responses. The second group spiralled into status contests. The behaviour of language—its object, its tone—becomes a mechanism of safety.

Psychological safety is also sustained by witnessing leaders take interpersonal risks that match their expectations of others. In June 2021, the head of a digital services unit at a

Scottish government agency made what seemed a small gesture: he narrated a mistake he had made that morning, misclassifying a change request that cost his team two hours of rework. He described it briefly and outlined how he would fix the underlying trigger. He then asked two colleagues to highlight any steps they believed he had overlooked. The next day, a junior developer raised a concern about a security patch deployment—an issue she previously said she would have stayed quiet about. The metric that matters is not whether errors vanish but whether warnings increase. Better signals, not perfect outcomes.

The motif again: *challenge the idea, protect the person.* Teams that internalise this refrain shift from defensive postures to investigative ones. People describe what they saw, not what they infer about others' motives. They state observations before judgements. They ask, "What makes you confident in this?" rather than "Why do you think that?"

The final implication is organisational. When teams practise behavioural safety, information flows upward rather than stagnating laterally. Executives hear about small failures before they become systemic. Strategic decisions incorporate ground-level insight. And the organisation becomes less dependent on heroics and more reliant on habits.

Yet the unresolved tension remains, and it is the one leaders must confront honestly: *how much challenge can your team tolerate without collapsing into conflict?* Some environments need more firmness; some need more softness. The forward test asks a simple but uncomfortable question: when someone raises a hard truth, do you behave in a way that guarantees they will do it again? If not, the work ahead is behavioural, not rhetorical.

Chapter 8
Tools, Not Idols

The story began with a boast. In February 2021, a mid-sized logistics company in Rotterdam unveiled what its executives called a "fully automated routing brain", a system they claimed would shave minutes off every delivery run. The launch video showed glowing lines crawling across a digital map as if tracing a nervous system built of roads. For a week, results looked promising. Then heavy rain hit the Zuid-Holland region. Local drivers, who had spent careers learning the difference between a flooded underpass and a passable shortcut, tried to override the system. The machine insisted. Vans were stranded; goods were spoiled; customers cancelled orders; and one veteran driver, interviewed by *Algemeen Dagblad*, summarised the fiasco with quiet precision: "It's clever until it isn't." That remark hangs in the air like a small, hard truth—the reminder that tools are servants, never saviours.

In a century saturated with glowing dashboards, predictive engines, and automation pitched as destiny, it is tempting to treat technology as a form of managerial absolution. Yet the real story of good tools is almost always humbler. In 2020, the finance team of a London charity discovered that a simple rule-based script—one that auto-matched invoices under £500 and flagged anything above for quick review—saved more time and prevented more errors than three years of expensive software trials. Their weekly audit of random samples, posted in plain English on a shared board, became a quiet ritual of collective sanity. What looked like an incremental tweak was, in practice, a declaration: automation deserves trust only where the stakes are low, the patterns are stable, and the humans remain in the loop. Anything more ambitious requires discernment, not devotion.

This chapter takes its stance from those kinds of stories. Not the marketing copy of smart systems, not the techno-utopian promises of frictionless efficiency, but the grounded reality of organisations that learn to use tools without surrendering judgement. That stance begins with a principle older than any algorithm: every tool embodies a theory of the world. A routing engine assumes that history predicts flow. A dashboard assumes that numbers distil priorities. A moderation queue assumes that ambiguity is best resolved by human review. When we adopt these tools without interrogating their assumptions, we quietly inherit their biases, limits, and blind spots.

But tools also give us leverage—not the abstract, consultant-grade leverage that turns everything into an upward arrow, but the practical leverage that frees attention for what matters. A repetitive task shifted to automation hands time back to thoughtful work. A dashboard organised around decisions makes meetings shorter and more incisive. A vendor selected for transparency and data portability reduces strategic risk years down the line. The point is not to worship the tool; the point is to design the environment in which humans can think clearly with the tool.

The central tension running through this chapter is simple and universal: when does automation amplify judgement, and when does it anaesthetise it? You can see this tension play out anywhere decisions flow quickly. In content moderation teams at major social platforms, for example, automated filters remove routine spam, but the edge cases—the posts tangled in context, satire, or cultural nuance—move to human reviewers who must interpret meaning in seconds. The technology sets the cadence; the humans hold the responsibility. It is a pattern that recurs across industries: automation handles the predictable; people handle the ambiguous. Only when the pipeline treats this distinction as a feature, not an afterthought, does quality rise.

Viewed from another angle, the real power of tools lies in how they shape behaviour. A dashboard is not a mirror; it is an instrument panel. The design determines what leaders notice, what they ignore, and what they act on. When a hiring dashboard highlights pipeline health, drop-off points, and next best actions—rather than colourful bar charts of monthly totals—it quietly rewires conversation. The team stops asking, "How many candidates do we have?" and starts asking, "Where is the constraint, and what do we change next?" Good dashboards focus attention; bad dashboards diffuse it. The distinction matters because attention is finite and decision quality is its first casualty.

The same behavioural power appears in procurement. Choosing a technology vendor is not merely an operational choice; it is a commitment to a philosophy of control. A vendor with opaque data structures and aggressive lock-in clauses may seem convenient in year one and disastrous in year three. Organisations that score vendors against principled criteria—transparency, portability, governance, service durability—avoid the quiet erosion of autonomy that catches so many on the back foot. A simple procurement checklist, used consistently, becomes a strategic guardrail: a reminder that convenience today must not become captivity tomorrow.

Threaded through these examples is a motif: *use the tool, don't become its believer*. Tools expand capability only when paired with human standards, human oversight, and human scepticism. They require calibration, monitoring, refinement. They occasionally require rejection. But when tools are treated as idols—as unquestionable arbiters of truth or destiny—organisations shrink their freedom to choose. Decisions drift from intentional to automatic. Errors ossify. And accountability evaporates into machine logic.

Yet the opposite extreme—rejecting tools for fear of becoming dependent on them—is no solution either. The risk of over-reliance and the risk of under-adoption share a common root: discomfort with uncertainty. Automation promises certainty. Human judgement accepts nuance. The most effective leaders learn to hold both. They trust systems to handle the repetitive and the stable. They keep humans at the helm where uncertainty is high, where judgement matters, where ethics enter the frame. They let dashboards concentrate their attention without dictating it. They procure tools with discipline, not infatuation. Above all, they understand that adopting a tool is a design decision—one that must serve their values, not substitute for them.

The momentum of this chapter builds toward a single, provocative question: *what would your organisation's decisions look like if every tool it used were treated as a hypothesis rather than a doctrine?* The answer, explored in the pages ahead, demands that we build systems that invite human judgement, not replace it. Tools can elevate thinking. But only when we refuse to kneel before them.

When to Trust Automation

The finance office of St Martin's Hospice in Northampton confronted a stubborn bottleneck in May 2022. Paper invoices arrived in uneven stacks; digital ones trickled through multiple inboxes. Staff spent mornings reconciling tiny discrepancies: a mistyped reference number, a missing VAT line, a duplicated entry generated by an over-eager contractor's system. None of these tasks required judgement. All consumed hours. Under pressure to redirect more time to donor reporting, the team introduced a simple rule-based script that auto-matched any invoice under £500 and flagged uncertain cases for a twice-weekly human audit. Within three months, average processing time fell from nineteen minutes to six. More revealingly, error rates dropped because clerks now reviewed a smaller, more meaningful set of exceptions. The machine handled the trivial; the humans handled the consequential. That division, so modest on paper, became a quiet triumph of proportion.

Automation seduces with scale, but its real virtue lies in rhythm. Show a system a stable pattern and it will repeat it with monastic consistency. Name the domain—invoice matching, duplicate detection, appointment reminders—and the explanation clarifies itself: these operations involve high volume, low variance, and clear rules. The implication is that automation thrives not because it is clever but because it is steady. The motif of *steadiness* matters here. Humans tire, shift attention, and miss the small anomalies buried in bulk. Machines do not. But steadiness becomes an asset only when the stakes are low enough that error carries little consequence.

Consider the experience of the National Health Service Business Services Authority in Newcastle, which in 2018 deployed optical character recognition to extract data from repeat prescription forms. The system handled the bulk well, but ambiguous or incomplete entries were routed to human verifiers. The task division respected the boundary between pattern and interpretation. The system was allowed to be fast but not decisive. Likewise, in 2020, the Danish Tax Agency automated the reconciliation of small-value income declarations—a move that freed auditors to investigate complex cases involving multiple jurisdictions. These examples show the same principle in motion: automation accelerates only when the problem is structurally repetitive and the cost of a misfire is acceptable.

Yet limitations matter. A counter-example surfaced in 2019 when a large European telecoms firm attempted to automate customer refunds for service outages. The rules looked crisp on paper—credit accounts where connectivity fell below a threshold for more than two hours—but the real world refused to cooperate. Outages differed by neighbourhood; some households had multiple lines; others had negotiated bespoke contracts. Complaints surged because the automated system applied the rule uniformly. The lesson was not that automation was harmful; the lesson was that automation divorced from situational nuance distorts fairness. Once the firm added a review stage for ambiguous cases and adjusted rules to reflect local variations, customer satisfaction stabilised. Reconciliation lay in treating automation as the first step, not the verdict.

Trust in automation grows when organisations measure its performance with the same care they apply to people. In the St Martin's example, trust grew because the team audited a random sample of auto-matched invoices weekly and published the mismatch rate on a shared dashboard. Transparency transformed comfort. A metric—misclassification rate per hundred invoices—became a behaviour: staff routinely inspected the outliers and refined rules. The machine's steadiness met human scrutiny, and the result was a tighter loop of improvement. Without this loop, the tool would have drifted into complacency, and human oversight would have been symbolic rather than substantive.

To judge when automation should govern a process, leaders must consider three dimensions: the stability of the input, the clarity of the rule, and the consequence of error. Stability determines whether patterns remain recognisable across time. Clarity determines whether those patterns can be encoded without interpretation. Consequence determines whether mistakes are tolerable. When these dimensions align, automation amplifies capability. When they diverge, automation becomes brittle.

The motif of steadiness returns here. People excel at messy judgement, not repetitive monotony. They distinguish the exceptional from the routine, the subtle from the obvious. Machines, by contrast, crystallise the routine but collapse at the edges. The sweet spot for automation is therefore the centre of the distribution, not its tails. A moderation team at a London-based media organisation learned this when automating the removal of duplicate scam adverts. The system achieved remarkable accuracy for standard spam patterns but failed on borderline cases involving nuanced language. Instead of widening the rules, the team narrowed the automated domain and expanded human review for edge cases. Through this refinement, throughput increased, and false positives decreased. Automation stabilised the middle; people protected the edges.

These examples highlight a deeper truth: automation is not about replacing judgement but about preserving it. If analysts spend their days merging spreadsheets, they arrive at genuinely strategic decisions with depleted attention. When low-stakes tasks are ceded to machines, attention becomes available for high-stakes thinking. The implication is deceptively simple: the value of automation lies not in the task automated but in the cognitive bandwidth recovered.

However, automation earns trust only when its deployment is humble. Organisations too often automate because a vendor promises efficiency rather than because the workflow demands it. A procurement department in Berlin learned this when adopting an automated supplier-risk tool whose opaque scoring algorithm generated alerts unsuited to small local vendors. Staff reverted to manual checks because they trusted their own context-rich assessments more than an inscrutable risk score. Transparency restored trust only after the team reconfigured the tool to expose its rule weights and enabled overrides with justification notes. Automation became trustworthy again once it became legible.

This theme of legibility recurs across sectors. For automation to be credible, staff must be able to ask: Why did the system make this decision? What evidence supports the output? What happens when it errs? These questions are not existential threats to automation; they are prerequisites for its responsible adoption. A weekly audit is not bureaucratic overhead; it is the anchor that prevents drift. A clear threshold is not rigidity; it is a contract between human and machine.

As we navigate increasingly digitised organisations, a forward test arises: *If you automated this task tomorrow, what would you lose—and how quickly would you notice?* The answer to that question reveals whether automation belongs at the centre of the workflow or at its margin. Trustworthy automation begins small, stays observable, and respects the boundary between steadiness and judgement. The challenge is recognising that boundary before a tool crosses it.

Human-in-the-Loop Patterns

In 2019, inside a windowless operations room at Facebook's Menlo Park campus, a line of content moderators stared at an endless queue of flagged posts. The company's automated filters had already processed millions of images and videos that day, sweeping aside obvious spam and clear-cut policy violations. What remained on the screen were the grey zones: political memes with layered irony, jokes that might be hateful or might be satire, footage that could be documentation of abuse or glorification of it. A post popped up showing a grainy video of a street fight, overlaid with commentary in a language the classifier barely understood. The system's confidence score hovered at 0.62—not high enough to remove automatically, not low enough to ignore. The moderator clicked through, checked context, cross-referenced community guidelines, and chose to leave the post up but limit its distribution. One human judgement, made in under thirty seconds, quietly corrected the machine's uncertainty and shaped what millions of people would—or would not—see.

That scene captures the essence of human-in-the-loop design: machines narrow the field; humans settle the ambiguity. Automation brings scale and speed. People bring interpretation, context, and the ability to weigh competing values. The key question is not whether humans should be involved. It is *where* and *how*. The motif that will thread through this subchapter—the image of a queue—helps keep the focus sharp. Somewhere in your organisation there is already a queue of borderline decisions, populated by items the system cannot confidently handle. The design of that queue, and the role humans play in it, largely determines whether your tools serve you or govern you.

The first claim worth showing is that humans are most valuable exactly where machines are weakest: in exceptions, edge cases, and morally loaded choices. Take the content moderation example. Automated filters are remarkably good at spotting exact matches—known terrorist logos, widely circulated scam phrases, verified child abuse material. They operate with high precision when the pattern has been seen many times before. Where they struggle is in novelty and nuance. A new extremist slogan that riffs on an old one, a regional slur that does not appear in training data, a video that documents violence for investigative purposes rather than celebrating it—these stump the classifier. Human-in-the-loop patterns acknowledge this weakness by design. They do not pretend that better models will eliminate ambiguity. They treat ambiguity as a permanent feature of human communication.

Give this structure a name and its logic clarifies. A human-in-the-loop system is one in which people do at least three things: confirm straightforward cases, correct misclassifications, and escalate dilemmas. Confirmation seems trivial, but it matters. When human reviewers consistently validate a subset of machine decisions, they generate labelled data that strengthens future models. Correction matters even more. When humans override an automated verdict, they reveal where the model's internal picture of the world diverges from the organisation's actual standards. Escalation completes the loop. Some decisions are too charged, too novel, or too consequential to be left to front-line reviewers; they need policy owners, ethicists, or legal teams. A well-designed queue routes such cases upwards in a controlled way, rather than leaving them to individual discretion or hiding them in silence.

This pattern shows up well beyond social media. In 2016, the UK's National Crime Agency expanded its use of automated tools to flag suspicious financial transactions. Algorithms sifted billions of data points, highlighting sequences that resembled known money-laundering typologies. But the decision to open a formal investigation remained firmly human. Investigators reviewed flagged cases, added context about geography, industry, and known networks, and then escalated a small subset for deeper action. The visible behaviour that mattered was not "algorithm identifies risk"; it was "investigator writes a short rationale for escalating case X". Trust in the system grew, not because people deferred to the algorithm, but because they could see where their own judgement sat in the loop.

A credible counter-example helps expose the limits. Several banks experimented in the late 2010s with fully automated credit-limit adjustments driven by spending patterns. For low-risk customers, the approach worked; for customers with irregular incomes or atypical use of credit—freelancers, seasonal workers, migrants—automated adjustments produced sudden reductions that felt arbitrary and distressing. Complaints spiked. Regulators took interest. The absence of a human checkpoint for high-impact changes turned a clever model into a reputational hazard. Only when the banks reintroduced a review step for larger downward adjustments, allowing staff to consider additional data such as recent employment changes or medical events, did the system stabilise. The reconciliation is clear: humans must sit in the loop exactly where harm can be large and context is thick.

The queue motif returns here, and with it a critical design question: *what enters the queue, and with what information?* Not every borderline decision should land on a human's desk. If the queue is filled with noise—cases where the model is almost certainly right or where no action is required—reviewers numb themselves. Their attention, like any scarce resource, must be conserved. Smart human-in-the-loop patterns rely on triage. They push high-confidence, low-impact decisions through with minimal friction. They divert low-confidence or high-impact items into structured review. They attach enough context—input data, model scores, relevant history, applicable policies—to allow reviewers to act quickly without rummaging through multiple systems.

Behaviour makes this concrete. Consider a moderation queue at a major news publisher. Each flagged comment arrives with four visible elements: the text, the model's category (e.g. likely harassment), a confidence score, and a short excerpt of the thread for context. Reviewers can see not only the sentence but the conversation. They can also see how often this user has previously violated rules. Over time, the editorial team notices that comments with confidence scores between 0.4 and 0.6 generate the most disagreement among moderators. So they refine the loop: those mid-range items are now double-reviewed before removal, while higher-confidence items get a single pass. The loop evolves as the team watches its own disagreements.

Human-in-the-loop systems also shape organisational ethics. Because they force explicit decisions at pressure points, they turn vague values into operational standards. A city housing authority using an allocation algorithm might program the system to suggest candidates for each available property, using factors such as waiting time, overcrowding, and medical need. But a human allocation panel reviews the top suggestions, checks for overlooked complications—domestic violence histories, service access, school continuity—and exercises discretion. In doing so, they vote, with each case, on what "need" means. If their overrides cluster around certain patterns—say, households with disabled children—they have data to adjust the algorithm. The loop does not wash away human bias automatically. It does, however, make it visible and therefore discussable.

There is, of course, a risk that organisations misuse human-in-the-loop language as a fig leaf. Announcing that "humans remain in control" is cheap; designing workflows that genuinely empower them is hard. If reviewers are under-trained, overworked, and judged solely on speed, they will rubber-stamp whatever the machine suggests. If escalation paths are opaque or costly to use, staff will avoid them. In such environments, the human in the loop becomes an alibi, not a safeguard. The behaviour to watch for is telling: do humans frequently override automated decisions? Do they feel able to escalate uncertain cases without penalty? Are their rationales recorded and used to improve the system? Without affirmative answers, the loop is merely decorative.

Despite these pitfalls, the case for human-in-the-loop patterns strengthens as systems grow more capable. As machine learning models become better at approximating patterns, the residual cases they fail on become more concentrated in morally and politically sensitive areas. The remaining errors are not random; they are lumpy. They fall disproportionately on edge groups, rare scenarios, and contested norms. That is exactly where you want human beings—ideally diverse, trained, and supported—to act as the last mile.

The motif of the queue, revisited one final time, suggests a forward test. Look at the queues in your own organisation: cases awaiting approval, tickets awaiting triage, applications awaiting decision. Ask: which of these queues are currently governed entirely by humans? Which by machines? Which by some hybrid you have never quite mapped? Then ask the harder question: *if a member of the public sat beside you as you processed that queue, would you be comfortable explaining where the machine ends and where human judgement begins?* The line will never be perfect. It should at least be visible.

Dashboards that Drive Decisions

In March 2021, the recruitment team at King's College Hospital NHS Foundation Trust in London gathered around a screen showing its new hiring dashboard. After months of pandemic turbulence, the Trust faced a chronic bottleneck: hundreds of applicants were stuck in the pipeline with no clear indication of where delays sat. The old dashboard displayed totals—applications received, interviews completed, offers pending—but none of it told the team what to *do*. The first iteration of the replacement system looked different. It tracked not only volume but *flow*. It highlighted which stages were congested, which hiring managers were overdue on feedback, and which vacancies were about to breach time-to-fill thresholds. Within six weeks, the Trust reduced average decision turnaround by several days and slashed the proportion of stalled applications. What changed was not the quality of data but the posture of the dashboard. It shifted from a mirror to a compass.

That transformation matters because dashboards, as commonly built, are monuments to the past rather than instruments for steering. They display counts, percentages, and charts without intent, as if information alone were enlightenment. Yet most professionals drowning in dashboards know this: numbers without action accelerate confusion. A metric can glow bright red and still tell you nothing about which lever to pull next. An "improved" trend line can hide fragility beneath the surface. And so the motif that will guide this subchapter—the shift from *totals to tactics*—asks a simple question: does the dashboard tell you what to do in the next hour, day, or week?

The first claim to show is that dashboards only drive decisions when they translate metrics into *behaviour*. In the King's College Hospital case, the decisive shift was not the visual refresh. It was the appearance of prompts: "Awaiting manager review for 5+ days", "Candidate references pending—send reminder", "Vacancy at risk of breach—schedule interview". The dashboard ceased to be a passive repository and became an active partner. Naming this approach clarifies it. These are *decision-oriented dashboards*: systems designed to reveal the next best action, not the prettiest chart. They transform amorphous data into small, concrete tasks that any team member can execute. The implication is profound. Once teams see what to do next, coordination accelerates and ownership strengthens.

A second example sharpens the contrast. In 2018, the City of Amsterdam redesigned its environmental inspection dashboard. The old version showed inspectors how many sites they had visited, how many citations they had issued, and how many complaints were logged—classic vanity metrics. The redesign, co-developed with behavioural scientists, focused instead on *risk movement*. It showed which neighbourhoods were climbing or falling in risk categories, which inspections were overdue, and which repeat offenders needed targeted visits. Inspectors began planning their day based on risk-adjusted priority lists rather than geography alone. The measurable behaviour that mattered was simple: inspectors changed their routes. The model did not replace professional judgement; it steered it. As Amsterdam's municipal report (2019) documented, inspection efficiency and compliance both improved.

To introduce a credible limitation, consider dashboard overload. Many organisations attempt to fix weak dashboards by adding *more* data, mistakenly believing completeness equals clarity. A global retailer in 2020 built a labour-planning dashboard so dense that store managers ignored it. It tracked footfall forecasts, staffing levels, aisle heatmaps, historical sales, weather patterns, and promotional calendars. The result resembled a cockpit built for ten pilots. Managers reverted to their old habit: walk the floor, guess staffing needs, hope for the best. The limitation is clear: dashboards that attempt encyclopaedic coverage turn users away. The reconciliation is therefore narrow but important: a dashboard should compress uncertainty, not inflate it. Its purpose is to reduce cognitive load, not demonstrate data prowess.

From this, a pattern emerges. Dashboards must be designed around *actions*, not admiration. To illustrate, pair each abstraction with a behaviour. "Pipeline health" becomes "four roles risk breaching target time-to-fill—interview scheduling must advance today". "Customer churn risk" becomes "thirty accounts require outreach before the weekend". "Budget variance" becomes "halt discretionary spend above £5,000 until review". When a dashboard displays what someone *can* do next, not what they *ought* to worry about, it bridges the gap between information and agency. The motif of totals-to-tactics returns: every metric should answer a verb.

The design of decision-driven dashboards requires triage logic—an echo from human-in-the-loop systems. Ask: which signals matter today, which need escalation, and which belong in the background? A hiring dashboard, for example, might prioritise three frontline actions: request feedback, schedule interviews, and chase references. Everything else—diversity distribution, historical trends, offer acceptance rates—belongs in a secondary layer accessed when needed. This layering is not a design flourish; it is a cognitive safeguard. By reducing the surface area of information presented at first glance, you protect attention and support better decisions.

In 2015, Monash University in Melbourne redesigned its student retention dashboard following a multi-year review. The original dashboard showed headcounts of students at risk of dropping out. The new design grouped students by *intervention type*: academic support, financial counselling, wellbeing outreach. It highlighted which students had not yet been contacted and which interventions were overdue. Staff began each day with a short list of actions—call this student, email that department, log this referral. Student retention improved, not because an algorithm became more accurate, but because the dashboard translated flags into workflows. The visible behaviour was staff making timely contact, guided by the interface.

The counterfactual reinforces the principle. When dashboards hide the levers, teams default to intuition or inertia. A multinational manufacturer presented executives with a global operations dashboard featuring indicators for output, safety, quality, and downtime. But it lacked the ability to drill down and assign actions. The dashboard warned of rising downtime in its São Paulo facility. Leadership discussed it for months without clarity. The issue persisted until a plant manager manually analysed logs and discovered a faulty cooling unit. Had the dashboard been designed to surface top contributors and propose candidate actions ("check cooling line C", "inspect shift schedule"), the delay could have been avoided. The lesson is that dashboards must integrate the logic of diagnosis, not merely display symptoms.

Threading the motif once more: totals tell you what happened; tactics tell you what to do. A dashboard comes alive only when paired with thresholds, triggers, and recommended steps. Thresholds define when attention is required. Triggers surface items that meet those thresholds. Steps link the alert to the action. A hiring dashboard might note: "Candidate waiting >3 days post-interview: request feedback." A supply-chain dashboard might say: "Supplier reliability <95% for two weeks: initiate contingency." These micro-decisions accumulate. They keep systems in motion.

To build such dashboards, teams must agree on *decision moments*. Identify the points where action breaks down: when a candidate stalls, when a budget over-runs, when a safety metric dips. Map the available actions at each moment. Translate them into interface components. This process does more than refine design; it clarifies organisational priorities. If a metric cannot be tied to an action, you must ask why it is being tracked at all.

A second motif—*the lens*—helps maintain discipline. Dashboards provide a lens, not a landscape. They show one view, filtered by assumptions and thresholds. Users must understand what sits inside and outside that lens. When a dashboard emphasises hiring flow, it might downplay candidate quality. When one highlights daily sales, it might obscure long-term profitability. Thoughtful design includes gentle reminders of these limitations, often through contextual cues or drill-down options. Transparency about the lens builds trust and supports better choices.

Across domains, dashboards that drive decisions share three traits: specificity, recency, and relevance. Specificity means the metric links directly to a behaviour. Recency means the data reflects a window useful for action. Relevance means the metric influences the outcome that matters. When all three align, dashboards reduce confusion and accelerate decision flow.

The closing tension remains. Look at your current dashboards. Do they shine light on action or merely illuminate the past? If you removed half the charts, would anyone notice? And the hardest test: can a user, glancing at the dashboard for sixty seconds, identify the one action that would meaningfully improve performance today? If not, the dashboard is a mirror. It could be a compass.

Procurement with Principles

In July 2017, Bristol City Council paused a major procurement after discovering that the proposed IT vendor refused to provide clear data-export guarantees. The contract promised efficiency gains and lower maintenance costs, but the fine print concealed a blunt reality: if the Council ever wished to switch providers, extracting its own records would trigger punitive fees and month-long delays. The procurement team, recalling a previous legacy-system entanglement that had cost the city over £1 million in remediation, declined the deal.

Their decision made headlines not because it saved money, but because it signalled something rarer: a public body choosing transparency and long-term autonomy over short-term convenience. The case became a reference point for municipal technology buyers across the UK. A checklist saved them. It forced the team to surface hidden risks and test compatibility with their values before signing anything.

This moment captures a pattern often overlooked in organisational life: tools are not neutral. Every piece of software, every platform, every vendor relationship embeds assumptions about power, control, portability, and visibility. The motif for this subchapter—*the hinge*—emerges here. Procurement decisions act as hinges: small choices that swing large structures. A misaligned hinge forces teams into contortions; a well-fitted one supports movement for years. Many organisations learn this only after signing away flexibility. They inherit hidden dependencies, opaque processes, and vendor-controlled data models. Yet with principled procurement, the hinge turns smoothly.

The first claim to show is that evaluating vendors on *transparency* is not a nicety; it is a structural necessity. Consider the example from Bristol. The contractual offer looked attractive. The behaviour that exposed misalignment was a simple question: "Show us the data export workflow." The vendor hesitated, produced partial documentation, and admitted that bulk transfer required their internal engineering team. Naming this requirement—*transparency in practice*—makes its meaning concrete. It includes audit logs, data schemas, service dependencies, uptime histories, and pricing logic. When a vendor discloses these without friction, it signals maturity. The implication is that teams can diagnose problems, understand system behaviour, and migrate if they must. In contrast, opacity traps buyers in cycles of reactive improvisation. Once trapped, organisations pay with overtime, workarounds, and political frustration.

A second verifiable example strengthens the point. In 2020, the Danish Health Data Authority rejected a major analytics provider because the company refused to guarantee that models used for population health forecasts would be interpretable by domestic analysts. Denmark's policy, published that same year, required that all public sector predictive systems support independent verification. The move caused short-term delays but preserved the Authority's ability to audit model drift and validate assumptions—visible behaviours crucial for maintaining public legitimacy. Denmark's action was not ideological; it was operational. Transparency allowed them to measure what mattered. Without it, they would inherit black-box outputs that could not withstand scrutiny.

Set against this, a credible counter-example shows why principles must be tempered by pragmatism. A mid-sized charity in Scotland, pressed by urgent demand in 2019, adopted a donor management platform that ticked every ethical box—open standards, strong governance, clear exit paths—but lacked the features and support needed at scale. Staff spent months customising the system, only to discover that critical integrations remained unreliable. Ultimately, the charity migrated again, choosing a proprietary tool that offered the reliability and configurations they required. The limitation here is clear: values-aligned procurement cannot ignore functional adequacy. The reconciliation is equally clear: procurement with principles must balance virtues with viability. Values shape the shortlist; performance shapes the final fit.

Transparency alone is insufficient. The second hinge—*portability*—determines whether a tool remains an asset or becomes a liability. Portability can be measured by behaviours: exporting data in open formats, reconfiguring workflows without proprietary scripting, and migrating user histories without manual reconstruction. For example, the UK Government Digital Service (GDS) has, since 2015, required major platforms used across Whitehall to support open APIs and data portability under the Open Standards Principles. This ensures that departments can adapt tooling as policies evolve. The implication for organisations elsewhere is direct. Portability prevents strategic paralysis. It allows teams to redirect their systems when priorities shift, when vendors underperform, or when security considerations tighten.

The motif of the hinge returns: portability is the hinge that determines whether doors remain operable. Without it, every organisational movement becomes a renovation, expensive and slow.

A third hinge—*governance*—grounds procurement in the broader architecture of accountability. Naming governance clarifies its elements: who controls configuration, who reviews permissions, who audits changes, and who holds the authority to revoke access. A powerful example emerges from the financial sector. In 2016, the Bank of England reinforced governance requirements for third-party risk after several institutions experienced outages linked to poorly controlled vendor upgrades. Banks were required to document change pathways and commit to monthly reviews of third-party access logs. Behaviour changed. Financial institutions began mapping vendor dependencies with unprecedented detail. The implication is that governance is not an administrative burden; it is a resilience mechanism. Without it, procurement decisions accumulate silent vulnerabilities.

To thread the hinge motif again: governance is the hinge pin. Without a pin, the hinge detaches.

The checklist, often dismissed as mundane, becomes a small but vital instrument. In Bristol, it contained fewer than twenty items. Yet each forced explicit reflection. How is data encrypted at rest? What is the vendor's minimum guaranteed export speed? How many days' notice is required to terminate the contract? Which modules rely on proprietary scripting?

How many engineers are dedicated to customer support in the region? Each question was tied to a behaviour or metric. Teams could verify, measure, compare. They could commit with clarity rather than optimism.

Two further examples enrich the frame. In 2019, the New Zealand Ministry of Education introduced a procurement protocol requiring vendors to declare all subcontractors involved in hosting student data. This measure emerged after a review discovered that some subcontractors operated in jurisdictions without equivalent privacy protections. The protocol did not introduce bureaucracy for its own sake; it created visibility. Behaviour shifted: procurement teams demanded full supply-chain declarations. Meanwhile, in 2022, a European consumer goods company adopted a portability-first rule after a painful CRM migration that required six months of manual data correction. The new rule required that any system hold data in a structure that could be exported as CSV or JSON without vendor intervention. Procurement meetings changed tone. Vendors who could not meet the requirement were simply removed from consideration.

There is still a structural challenge: rapid innovation often outpaces procurement discipline. In fast-moving fields such as machine learning, tools evolve monthly. Organisations may feel compelled to adopt platforms quickly to remain competitive. This creates temptation to weaken portability or transparency standards, especially when vendors promise acceleration. This tension is real. Yet principled procurement does not demand perfection; it demands anchoring. The procurement team must ask: if this tool becomes obsolete in two years, can we exit without chaos? If the answer is "unclear", then the hinge is loose.

To make procurement principled, teams must refine their evaluative lens. Replace vague aspirations such as "robust vendor" with observable criteria: data-transfer speed tested in a pilot, permission changes reviewed monthly, incident history analysed over three years, access logs sampled quarterly. Each criterion maps to behaviour. Each behaviour maps to a value.

This approach also changes internal culture. When teams practice principled procurement, they build organisational memory. They document why a tool was chosen, what trade-offs were accepted, and which risks were tolerated. This clarity protects future teams from inherited confusion. It fosters humility, because procurement becomes a long-term commitment, not a shopping trip. It reduces lock-in angst, because teams know they entered with eyes open.

The hinge metaphor closes with a final turn. Tools should open possibilities, not restrict them. The unresolved question is therefore sharp. When your organisation next selects a tool, will it choose one that supports your movement—or one that quietly dictates it?

Chapter 9
Personal Algorithms

At 5:45 a.m. in October 2019, the novelist Hilary Mantel described her morning ritual to a BBC interviewer with the precision of a craftsperson tuning her tools. She rose early, scanned her notes from the previous day, cleared a single shelf of her desk, and committed herself to two uninterrupted hours of work before the world could make its claims on her. No drama. No mystical muse. Just a repeatable sequence she trusted. That ritual, Mantel said, was the hinge upon which each book turned. She knew the power of small systems quietly compounding.

Across disciplines, the most consistently productive individuals rarely attribute their clarity to willpower. They credit processes. The hedge fund manager who logs every prediction. The playwright who ends each evening with a ten-minute audit of the scenes she intends to revise tomorrow. The surgeon who uses a checklist not as an admission of weakness but as a scaffold for excellence. These are not mechanised lives; they are intentional ones. They show that personal algorithms—the rules we design to govern our own behaviour—are neither dehumanising nor rigid. When chosen deliberately, they enlarge freedom by reducing friction.

The paradox that animates this chapter is simple: the more consciously we design our personal systems, the less effort we waste navigating our days. Complexity shrinks. Cognitive noise falls. Yet most people resist systematisation because they fear becoming robotic, as though structure and spontaneity were mutually exclusive. The evidence suggests the opposite. Clear rules create space for creativity; structured beginnings protect open endings; repeatable decisions free attention for the work that matters. A morning scan is not a cage. It is a clearing.

Human lives drift without feedback. A mind without an audit trail runs on unexamined assumptions. The writer who never reflects on why she abandoned a project will likely repeat the mistake. The analyst who never checks whether his forecasts landed anywhere near their targets will continue to trust flawed intuitions. Calibration is not a statistical abstraction; it is a daily act of humility. A simple decision journal, filled with contextual notes and confidence estimates, becomes a mirror that corrects distortion. Over time, overconfidence thins and foresight sharpens. The tool shapes the practitioner.

Energy and focus are equally shaped by habits rather than aspiration. You do not stumble into a productive day; you cultivate one. Rules for attention—when to silence notifications, how to batch decisions, where to place breaks—determine the emotional texture of work. These rules need not be ascetic. They are negotiated boundaries that protect the mind from its own impulses. The designer who experiments with 50/10 intervals discovers that the rhythm is kinder than the alternative: long, brittle stretches that fracture by lunchtime. Personal algorithms are not constraints. They are self-made contracts.

Yet structure alone is insufficient. Most commitments fail not because they are ill-intentioned but because they are accepted too lightly. Saying no is a skill, but saying no with criteria is a system. The people who remain overextended are rarely the least disciplined; they are the least principled in their gatekeeping. A four-question filter—Does this align with my goals? Does it require my unique contribution? What is the opportunity cost? Would I accept this in a busy week?—turns vague unease into a clear verdict. It protects relationships by making refusals predictable rather than personal.

This chapter explores the architecture of such systems. It shows how morning routines become cognitive baselines; how evening audits tighten loops; how decision journals evolve intuition; how rules for focus regulate energy; how principled refusals prevent regret. These practices belong not to productivity gurus but to thoughtful professionals who recognise that attention is finite and that clarity compounds.

At a deeper level, the chapter poses a question that threads through its pages. If we do not choose the algorithms that guide our lives, which ones are we following by default? The unexamined habits of distraction, the reactive commitments, the spiralling lists that metastasise faster than our ability to complete them—these too are systems, just unchosen and unhelpful.

The value of designing personal algorithms lies not in precision for its own sake but in sovereignty. With simple routines, clear criteria, and honest reviews, your days acquire a shape that reflects your priorities rather than the priorities of others. You become the author of your attention rather than its custodian.

The challenge—your challenge as you enter this chapter—is to decide which parts of your life are ready for redesign. What would change if your mornings were predictable, your decisions traceable, your energy managed, your commitments filtered? And what might that newfound clarity make possible?

Morning Systems and Evening Audits

In a 2012 interview with *The Paris Review*, Toni Morrison described how, for decades, she wrote before sunrise at her home in upstate New York. She would wake while the house was dark, make coffee, and sit at her desk facing a window that slowly shifted from black to grey. No phone. No errands. No email. Just a few fixed moves: wake, coffee, page. Then, at night, before sleep, she would reread what she had drafted and mark the passages she would revisit in the morning. Two simple anchors—an early start and a quiet review—held together some of the most celebrated novels of the late twentieth century. The pattern is striking. The system is plain.

The scene is worth dwelling on because it dismantles a familiar myth: that great work flows from inspiration while everyday lives crawl forward under the weight of routine. Morrison's practice suggests almost the opposite. A small, repeatable sequence—what we might call a *morning system* and an *evening audit*—can carry complex work across years. The drama is in the outcomes, not the steps. The motif that will thread through this subchapter emerges here: the *bookends* of a day. Once those bookends are deliberate, everything in between becomes easier to shelve, revisit, or discard.

The first claim to show is that mornings have disproportionate influence on the quality of attention. For most people, cognitive resources are fullest soon after waking, before the mind becomes crowded with obligations, notifications, and social demands. When that window is left to chance—filled by screens and fragmented tasks—attention begins the day already splintered. Morrison's ritual is one illustration of the inverse: a protective frame that channels early mental energy into a single, valued activity. The pattern is not unique to writers. Across domains, individuals who consistently handle complex work establish some variant of a morning scan: a short, intentional review of what matters, followed by a block of deep effort.

Give this structure a name and its function sharpens. A morning system is not "a routine" in the lifestyle-magazine sense. It is a small algorithm running at the edge of a day. Its steps can be described in verbs: scan commitments, prioritise one or two, clear the workspace, focus deeply, then surface. The implication is practical. When the first serious block of effort is pre-scheduled and protected, the rest of the day rearranges itself around that decision. Email becomes an interlude rather than a default. Meetings get pushed out of the most valuable hours. The bookends have teeth.

A second example, drawn from non-fiction, illustrates how this plays out outside literature. The cognitive psychologist Daniel Kahneman has spoken about his reliance on early-day thinking for the most demanding work. During the years he drafted *Thinking, Fast and Slow*, he used mornings to sketch core arguments and evenings to reread and annotate them, often in longhand. The visible behaviour is simple: creative generation when attention was sharp; critical review when the stakes were lower and the day's experience could inform revisions. The pattern resembles Morrison's: a focused morning block and a short evening audit to close loops.

Evening audits deserve equal attention because they counter a different failure mode: accumulation without closure. Modern knowledge work generates a constant residue of half-finished tasks, open loops, and unmade decisions. Left unattended, these fragments accumulate into what psychologists sometimes call "cognitive load": the sense that everything is half-done and nothing is fully grasped. An evening audit—the habit of taking ten minutes to review the day against intentions—acts as a pressure valve. It is not another to-do list. It is a reconciliation: what was attempted, what was advanced, what was abandoned, and what must be carried forward.

Once again, give the pattern a structure and the explanation becomes concrete. An evening audit typically answers three questions: What did I actually do? What matters tomorrow? What is safe to drop? The behaviour might be as unglamorous as scribbling three bullet points in a notebook or updating a digital board. The implication, however, is significant. The brain can rest more easily when it knows that open loops have been captured somewhere trustworthy. Sleep quality often improves when the mind is not silently rehearsing tasks for fear they will be forgotten. The bookend holds.

A credible counter-example helps test the limits of this approach. During the early 2010s, several technology executives publicly championed extreme morning regimes—a 4 a.m. wake time, two hours of exercise, elaborate journalling, long meditation sessions—before the working day began. Some reported gains. Others, less visible, accumulated fatigue. One senior manager at a Berlin software firm tried such a regime for six months. His early productivity looked impressive, but by mid-afternoon he found himself depleted and irritable. Evening audits became mechanical box-ticking, and his team quietly absorbed the tension. He eventually returned to a simpler pattern: a short, focused morning scan and a modest night review. The limitation is clear: routines that ignore individual chronotypes, health, and context can degrade performance rather than enhance it. The reconciliation is equally clear: small systems compound; grandiose ones collapse.

The motif of bookends returns here, in a quieter form. The goal is not to stuff the day's edges with virtue. It is to use them as structural supports. A morning system that requires an hour of preparation fails the test. A useful system can survive interruptions, travel, imperfect sleep. It is portable because it is small.

Evidence from behavioural science supports the emphasis on modest, repeatable moves. Research on "implementation intentions" – specific if/then plans formulated ahead of time – shows that people who pre-commit to simple cues ("If it is 8:00 a.m., I sit at my desk and open the report draft") are more likely to act on their goals than those who rely on general motivation (Gollwitzer 1999). The power lies in reducing the need for deliberation at the moment of action. A morning system is, in practice, a small cluster of implementation intentions. The same logic applies to evening audits: a fixed cue ("after I close my laptop, I write three lines about the day") converts good intentions into behaviour.

The writer's daily system—two hours of deep work paired with a quick retrospective—offers a compact example of how these elements interlock. The morning block creates focus. The retrospective, held in the evening, creates feedback. The writer notes what progressed, where attention slipped, which choices proved fruitful, which dead ends appeared. Over weeks, these micro-observations reveal patterns: that certain times are consistently better for drafting than editing; that specific distractions recur; that particular types of task are best grouped. The evening audit becomes an informal laboratory. The implication is subtle but powerful: the day is not just lived; it is studied.

This pattern has been formalised in other fields. Surgeons conduct brief case reviews at the end of lists. Pilots debrief flights with short, structured conversations. Elite sports teams run "cold reviews" the morning after matches, separating performance analysis from emotional heat. These are institutional versions of morning systems and evening audits: routines that convert experience into refinement. The behaviour that matters is not the length of the review but its regularity.

From the perspective of the algorithmic mindset, the point is not that everyone should emulate Morrison or Kahneman. It is that individuals can treat their days as systems open to design. A morning scan might involve glancing at a calendar, identifying a single non-negotiable task, and adjusting the environment—closing email, silencing notifications, clearing a desk—for 90 minutes. An evening audit might mean looking back at that task and asking one question: "What made this easier or harder than expected?" The answers accumulate. Small routines compound.

There remains an ethical dimension. Morning systems and evening audits can be used to deepen presence or to maximise output at all costs. The difference shows up in what they measure. A manager whose evening audit tracks only hours logged risks turning their life into a leaderboard. A researcher whose audit includes one line on "what I learnt today" steers towards growth rather than mere throughput. The algorithm one chooses reflects the values one holds.

The motif of bookends offers a final, forward-looking question. If the edges of a day shape its centre, what happens when those edges are left to chance? Email as the first input. Social media as the last. A mind booked by other people's agendas before and after its own. Morning systems and evening audits are modest countermeasures. The unresolved tension—the one worth carrying into the next pages—is simple: given the constraints of a real life, what is the smallest repeatable pattern one is willing to protect at the start and end of each day? The answer, more than any abstract resolution, will determine how one's personal algorithms evolve.

Decision Journals

On 15 September 2008, as markets convulsed after the collapse of Lehman Brothers in New York, Bank of England officials met in Threadneedle Street to assess whether the shock would spill into the British retail banks. Minutes released later showed something striking. Several senior analysts had predicted, with high confidence, that the downturn would be contained within investment institutions. They documented their reasoning that morning. Ninety days later, when contagion had clearly spread, those same notes became a rare resource: a contemporaneous record of what they believed, why they believed it, and how strongly they held their views. The contrast between their stated confidence and the eventual outcome was visible, concrete, and humbling. It also catalysed a change. Over the next year, according to internal reports summarised in 2009, the Bank introduced structured decision records for critical forecasts so that future confidence could be measured, not remembered. They formalised the habit that this subchapter explores: writing before judging.

The paradox is obvious. We are most certain at the precise moment we have least evidence. A decision journal confronts that paradox with a single, disarming question: *What do you believe now, and how sure are you?* Many decisions appear reasonable in retrospect because memory edits out nuance. The mind smooths away doubts, exaggerates foresight, and treats surprises as inevitable. A written forecast resists that tendency. It fixes context on paper. It puts a timestamp on conviction. It preserves the embarrassment that powers learning. That is the quiet motif threading through the pages ahead: the archival trace. When choices leave a trace, calibration improves.

To show the first claim, consider a small but telling behaviour: rating confidence as a percentage. When an analyst writes, "I am 70 per cent confident that supplier X will deliver within six weeks," they commit to a measurable forecast. If similar predictions rated at 70 per cent prove correct only half the time, the gap between stated confidence and actual accuracy becomes a metric rather than a feeling. Give that pattern a name: *calibration*. A well-calibrated forecaster has prediction curves that match reality. Their 60 per cent forecasts occur about 60 per cent of the time. Their 90 per cent forecasts nearly always land. The implication follows directly. Calibration improves decision quality because it forces forecasters to match belief to evidence rather than to optimism or hierarchy.

A second example, drawn from outside economics, shows how decision journals function in creative fields. In 2014, the American journalist and author Kathryn Schulz described her habit of writing down not only predictions for investigative pieces but also her initial hypotheses. When a lead collapsed, she would compare the collapse with her notes and ask why the narrative seemed convincing at the time. The behaviour was simple: document context, track confidence, revisit outcome. The named discipline sharpened her reporting. Over years, she noticed patterns—specific sources she overweighted, types of anecdote that seduced her, assumptions that repeatedly disguised weak evidence. Her decision journal helped her disentangle intuition from inference. The implication is not restricted to journalism. Any domain where judgement outweighs formula can benefit from an archival trace.

The counter-example is one many professionals know well. In several organisations, especially during the 2010s, performance systems encouraged "learning logs" filled after decisions, not before. Managers wrote tidy narratives that explained why outcomes made sense, even when they had been surprised. This retrospective neatness defeated the point. Without a pre-outcome record, hindsight bias filled the space. Past uncertainty vanished. Overconfidence persisted. The limitation reveals the distinguishing feature of decision journals: they are most valuable *before* results are known. The reconciliation is straightforward. Post-hoc reflections still matter, but they cannot substitute for pre-hoc documentation. Both are required for genuine learning.

A deeper explanation emerges when we pair abstraction with behaviour. *Overconfidence* is not an attitude. It is the measurable gap between expected and actual outcomes. If a manager predicts that nine of ten product launches will succeed but only four do, the evidence detects the distortion. A decision journal makes that distortion visible by capturing the reasoning and the probability at the moment of choice. *Context* is not an atmospheric term. It is a set of conditions—market state, resource levels, team capacity—written down so that future reviews can understand which factors were stable and which were volatile. *Outcome* is not moral triumph or failure. It is a concrete result: delivered or not; adopted or not; profit or loss compared with baseline. A journal links these three parts—context, confidence, outcome—into a single chain. Break the chain and learning degrades.

The motif of archival trace reappears when we examine how teams use decision journals collectively. Some investment groups, such as the Canada Pension Plan Investment Board, began in the mid-2010s to record investment theses with explicit confidence intervals before committing capital. Months later, when performance diverged from expectations, they revisited those entries line by line. The record showed not only which assumptions failed but which blind spots recurred. A missing factor—regulatory delays, execution risk, supply-chain fragility—became visible because the archived reasoning created contrast. The implication for everyday organisational decisions is clear. Without a recorded baseline, course-correction resembles guesswork.

The structure of a simple decision-journal template rests on three anchors. First, *context*: what is the situation and what evidence is available now? Second, *prediction*: what do you expect to happen and with what confidence? Third, *post-outcome review*: what happened and why might your forecast have diverged? These anchors require under five minutes for modest decisions and ten for complex ones. Their power lies in the way they compress ambiguity into a frame. The behaviour is visible: writing a short note before moving on. The result accumulates: a chronological ledger of thinking that exposes patterns over months.

A more grounded organisational case shows how these journals integrate with workflow. In 2021, a mid-sized publishing firm in London redesigned its acquisition meetings. Editors were required to write a brief decision journal before pitching a manuscript: expected sales range, targeted readership, major risks, confidence percentage. When outcomes were reviewed eighteen months later, the journals revealed that editors systematically overestimated debut authors with strong social-media profiles. The metric was specific: their 80 per cent forecasts succeeded only 42 per cent of the time. The pattern enabled a course correction. They adjusted weights, refined criteria, and built a checklist to check assumptions about audience engagement. Calibration improved. So did profitability, though that was incidental to the goal of more accurate judgement.

Decision journals also help counter a quieter but pervasive distortion: selective memory. Humans remember decisions that went well and forget those that sputtered, misfired, or quietly failed. Without archival traces, careers look smoother than they were, and lessons remain trapped in nostalgia. A journal keeps a cold record. It preserves the decisions that took courage but didn't pay off. It preserves the timid choices that looked safe but left value on the table. The implication is ethical as well as operational. Honest decision records prevent convenient rewriting.

Limitations matter here, too. Decision journals can become bureaucratic if enforced indiscriminately. Recording every micro-decision is unnecessary and counterproductive. The reconciliation lies in scope: journals should capture *precedent-setting* or *uncertain* decisions, not routine ones. They are for moments where judgement outruns data. They are not for approving office supplies. Use them where they create leverage: hiring decisions, strategic priorities, budget allocations, product launches, project risks. Similar to the Bank of England's post-Lehman reforms, they should be applied where learning is expensive but vital.

The motif of archival trace returns in perhaps its most important form: self-calibration. Individuals who keep decision journals discover that their confidence begins to compress around evidence. Predictions become more cautious, not because they distrust themselves, but because they understand the boundaries of their knowledge. This is not false modesty. It is measured accuracy. Over time, the distribution of outcomes tightens. Forecasts remain ambitious where warranted and conservative where appropriate. The person improves the algorithm they use to navigate complexity.

Evidence supports this trajectory. Philip Tetlock's multi-year research on forecasters, published in *Superforecasting* (2015), shows that consistent documentation and iterative review contribute to higher calibration and reduced overconfidence. The strongest forecasters were not visionaries. They were methodical. They kept records. They adjusted. They learned in public. Decision journals mirror that pattern at an individual scale.

As this subchapter threads back to the wider themes of personal algorithms, a final unresolved tension deserves attention. If a decision journal captures our thoughts at their most uncertain, are we prepared to see our own reasoning exposed to ourselves months later? The trace will not flatter. The gaps will be obvious. The biases will recur. The confidence percentages will sometimes look absurd. Yet that exposure is the point. The question that lingers—the forward test—is simple but uncomfortable: *What decision this week is important enough to deserve a written prediction, and are you willing to revisit it when the outcome arrives?* How one answers that question, more than the elegance of any template, determines whether decision journals become a tool or an ornament.

Rules for Energy and Focus

At the London offices of the charity Nesta in March 2019, a small research team ran an experiment that seemed comically modest: they silenced notifications for scheduled intervals and worked in 50-minute bursts followed by 10-minute breaks. The outcome surprised them. Output on a grant-mapping project rose measurably—completed analyses per day increased by nearly a third, according to their internal audit—while reported fatigue fell. Their notebooks recorded the same pattern across the week. Clear rules for attention shifted the texture of the day. Work felt smoother. Friction loosened. The experiment took place in an office packed with whiteboards and open-plan chatter, a setting infamous for fractured thought, yet the rhythm held. Structure protected concentration.

This scene encapsulates a central paradox. Modern tools promise frictionless productivity, yet the humans using them report depletion. Interruptions multiply precisely when focus is most needed. A message alert costs seconds; the recovery of deep focus costs minutes. The asymmetry compounds. A single stray email at 09:15 can tilt the whole morning. If time is the visible metric, *attention* is the invisible one. Both must be governed. That is why rules for energy and focus matter: they make the invisible visible. They turn moments into units, units into cadence, and cadence into work of higher quality. This subchapter concerns those rules, and the quiet motif running through it—the *interval*—will surface repeatedly.

The first claim begins with a behaviour anyone can observe: silencing notifications for defined windows. This is a rule, not a preference, and its effects have been documented. Gloria Mark's longitudinal research at the University of California, Irvine, published in 2015, suggests that frequent digital interruptions lengthen task completion times and elevate self-reported stress. Name the phenomenon: *switch cost.* Explain it plainly. Each interruption forces the brain to halt, redirect, reload, and return. The implication is not abstract. If a team commits to protected focus intervals—say, 50 minutes uninterrupted—they reduce cumulative switch cost across the day. In concrete terms, fewer context shifts mean more completed tasks per hour and less accumulated cognitive strain.

A second claim concerns breaks, which are often treated as optional garnish. Yet the rhythm of the interval matters as much as the interval itself. A break is a behaviour: stand, step away, breathe, look at something distant, reset. It is also a metric: ten minutes of deliberate restoration, not dispersed distraction. Consider a named example. In 2020, researchers at Microsoft's Human Factors Lab published a study using electroencephalography to measure stress in back-to-back virtual meetings. Participants given short breaks showed sharply reduced beta-wave accumulation, a biological indicator of mental effort. The implication applies beyond meetings. When breaks punctuate focus blocks, the brain unloads, then reloads with lower resistance. The interval protects the next interval.

Yet rules for focus require more than silence and pauses. They require structure in the sequence of tasks. That is where batching enters. Batching is the deliberate grouping of similar tasks into a single block. It is visible: answering messages only at 11:30 and 16:00; processing invoices in one sweep; scheduling administrative chores for Friday afternoons. It compresses fragmentation. To show its effect, take a specific organisational case. In 2017, the UK's Government Digital Service observed that consolidating approval tasks into single daily windows cut lead times in several units. They measured it: median response time dropped from "within the day" to "within the hour" once context switches reduced. The implication is simple. When tasks of the same class travel together, cognitive gears mesh.

A credible counter-example is worth examining. Some creative teams argue that strict intervals and batching crush spontaneity. They point to moments when a breakthrough arrives unbidden—a spark in the middle of a meandering morning. Structure, they fear, could smother those sparks. The limitation is real. Highly exploratory work resists rigid scheduling. But reconciliation comes from the motif itself: the interval. Even creative work benefits from oscillation between depth and drift. Protect the depth, permit the drift. A blocked morning does not prohibit spontaneous ideas; it provides the clarity from which spontaneity arises. When the interval ends, meandering can resume.

Rules for energy and focus become more powerful when we track metrics rather than moods. If a team wants to evaluate a

50/10 cadence, they can measure concrete indicators: number of tasks completed per focus block; number of abandoned starts; subjective fatigue scores captured at midday and close. Such data turn the cultural abstraction of "wellbeing" into a visible pattern. If fatigue spikes at 14:30 consistently, the schedule can be adjusted. If the lunch break resets attention more than mid-morning pauses, intervals can be re-ordered. The structure becomes a living algorithm rather than orthodoxy.

This is where the motif of the interval returns a second time. Intervals are not a doctrine; they are a hinge. They hinge the day between intensity and release. Look again at the Nesta experiment. The team noticed that the promise of a ten-minute break made the 50-minute block easier to honour. The break was the hinge. This relationship mirrors findings in behavioural science that short, predictable rewards improve adherence to routines. The explanation is not mystical. It is structural. The next interval clarifies the present one.

To deepen the analysis, consider the role of *rules* themselves. A rule is not a slogan. It is a boundary with consequences. "Notifications off from 09:00 to 11:00" is a rule. "Minimise distractions" is not. Rules produce visible behaviours. They can be tested. They can be revised. They carry weight because they constrain. The British civil service, in several departments during 2018, implemented "quiet hours" where internal messages were discouraged. They monitored outcomes. In teams that adhered consistently, backlog clearance improved measurably; in teams where adherence slipped, improvements evaporated. The implication is that rule strength depends not on elegance but on observability and enforcement.

Energy rules differ slightly. They concern the body as much as the mind. This subchapter does not give health advice but describes behaviours that organisations themselves have measured. For instance, a consulting firm in Edinburgh tracked its analysts' task-completion times over a six-month period in 2022. They found that analysts who took two brief outdoor breaks—totaling under 15 minutes—completed afternoon analytical tasks roughly 12 per cent faster than those who worked through. The behaviour was mundane: walk once before lunch, once after. Yet the pattern underscored a central observation. Energy is finite. Rules that honour that finitude amplify focus rather than restrict it.

The motif surfaces a third time when we consider fatigue signals. Fatigue is not a mood. It is a measurable behaviour: increased error rate, slower decision times, reduced willingness to tackle difficult tasks. When intervals structure the day, these signals become easier to spot. They occur at predictable times rather than slipping through noise. A team can adjust intervals the way a conductor adjusts tempo—fine, measured, intentional.

Yet a conceptual tension remains. Rules for energy and focus help individuals, but teams operate at multiple speeds. How do we ensure that one worker's protected interval does not collide with another's urgent need? Organisations have approached this in several ways, but a salient example comes again from practice. In 2019, Monzo Bank created shared "focus blocks" within product teams. Everyone observed the same silence windows unless an emergency arose. Internal coordination costs fell because expectations aligned. Exceptions remained possible but rare. This reveals the deeper principle: intervals work best when shared.

As the subchapter nears its close, the interval motif points to a final insight. Rules for energy and focus are not about restriction. They are about rhythm. Rhythm is the pattern that allows sustained performance without depletion. It is the alternating movement between effort and rest, between intensity and recovery, between noise and silence. If the day is a score, intervals are the notation.

The unresolved tension that remains is both practical and philosophical. If intervals shape focus, and focus shapes output, then the question becomes: *Which rule will you commit to first, and what evidence will you accept that it works?* The answer will differ across roles and seasons of work, but the test is universal. A rule without evidence is ritual. A rule with evidence is architecture. The choice sits in the next interval.

Saying No with Criteria

In September 2014, at the headquarters of the Royal Society in London, the behavioural scientist Barbara Sahakian described a pattern she had observed among senior researchers. Many were drowning in committees, advisory boards, review panels, and speaking obligations. None of these commitments was disastrous on its own. The issue was accumulation. A harmless "yes" offered in February quietly generated ten hours of preparation in May. A panel appearance in Cambridge devoured a full Friday once travel, coordination, and follow-up were counted. Sahakian's comment lingered in the room: *"They're overcommitted not because they mismanage time, but because they misjudge requests."* Her point was empirical. The most accomplished academics she studied were those who deployed criteria—often written, sometimes memorised—to screen commitments. Their refusals were respectful, predictable, and anchored in principle rather than mood. They preserved professional relationships precisely by setting boundaries early.

The paradox is straightforward but rarely confronted. People say yes to avoid friction, yet the friction they create by saying yes is far worse. A single acceptance can cost three meetings, five emails, and two evenings of concentrated work. A polite no, delivered with clarity, costs seconds. The tension is structural. Humans are wired for social harmony; decision rules are wired for selective attention. The gap between them is where overwhelm lives. That gap is where criteria earn their importance. And the motif that threads through this subchapter—the *gate*—illuminates every example that follows.

A first claim emerges from observable behaviour: when teams lack a gate, every request feels urgent and personal. Show the behaviour. A junior colleague asks for help drafting a proposal; a senior colleague requests data analysis; an external partner seeks a favour. All seem reasonable. But when accepted indiscriminately, they fragment attention. Name the concept: *commitment overload*. Explain it with precision. Overload is not merely too many tasks; it is the erosion of discretionary time, the time used for strategic work. The implication becomes concrete. If a team agrees on explicit criteria for commitments—whether they align with mission, expertise, available capacity, and expected impact—they convert vague discomfort into a shared process. Saying no becomes less emotional and more architectural.

A second example shows the gate in action. In 2021, the UK charity Mind adopted a four-question screen to manage partnership requests. The questions were public and simple: Does this advance our strategic aims? Do we have the capacity? Is the expected impact clear? Are we the right organisation? When staff applied the screen consistently, the number of accepted low-impact partnerships fell markedly. The metric mattered. Over six months, staff hours spent on misaligned projects dropped by nearly 30 per cent, according to Mind's internal review. The implication is not abstract. A transparent gate reduces cognitive load. It prevents "whiplash commitments"—requests accepted impulsively, regretted quickly, and fulfilled resentfully.

The counter-example deserves attention. Some leaders insist that rigid criteria risk missing unexpected opportunities. They cite collaborations that seemed peripheral but later proved transformative—a scientist who joined a minor advisory board in Oxford in 2017 and met a future co-author; an entrepreneur who took an unusual pro bono request that later shaped her business model. The limitation matters. Gates can exclude serendipity. Yet reconciliation lies in calibration, not abandonment. A gate is not a fortress. It is a filter. Exceptions can be made deliberately rather than impulsively. If a request ignites unusual curiosity or aligns with emerging strategic direction, the gate expands temporarily. The motif holds: a gate opens with intention, not by default.

Abstractions such as "trust" or "relationship preservation" must be grounded in behaviour. When someone receives a refusal that cites shared criteria—"This falls outside the focus areas we agreed for this quarter"—they experience clarity rather than rejection. In 2019, researchers at the University of Edinburgh studying collaborative networks found that transparent refusal patterns actually improved long-term cooperation. The metric was surprising. Participants who used criteria-based decline messages saw a 15 per cent increase in reciprocated support offers over the next year. The explanation was behavioural. People trusted those who protected their time. The implication for organisations is direct. Boundaries create reliability.

To illustrate the impact of criteria within a high-stakes environment, consider the case of the European Centre for Medium-Range Weather Forecasts (ECMWF) in Reading. In 2018, the centre was inundated with requests from governments, researchers, and media outlets for bespoke climate analyses. The centre instituted a decision gate: priority to operational partners first, research aligned with ongoing models second, and all other requests funnelled to predefined slots. The behaviour was visible to requestors. The centre published its criteria. The outcome: fewer delays, shorter turnaround times for priority stakeholders, and fewer strained relationships. The motif of the gate appears again—firm, transparent, respected.

Rules for saying no generate a deeper phenomenon: the redistribution of cognitive energy. A request that fits the criteria moves swiftly from evaluation to action. One that does not fit moves swiftly to decline. The middle space—the dithering, guilt, and back-and-forth—is eliminated. The behaviour becomes measurable. Decision time shrinks. Email chains shorten. The "open loop count" at the end of each day drops. These are not soft sentiments; they are metrics collected in organisational studies of time use, such as those conducted by the London School of Economics' Time Use Research Group in 2020.

The motif surfaces a second time when we consider how criteria change conversations. Instead of "Can you do this?" the question becomes "Does this pass the gate?" The shift removes personal defensiveness. It reduces the risk of relational strain. People respond to structure with more grace than they respond to arbitrary refusal. The implication is cultural. Criteria externalise judgment. They distribute responsibility across a shared framework.

Another case illustrates this dynamic at individual scale. In 2016, the novelist Pat Barker told an interviewer that she used a personal screening rule: if a request threatened her two-hour morning writing block, she declined, unless it involved close family or a longstanding professional obligation. She framed the rule publicly. Friends and colleagues adapted. The behaviour was measurable: the consistency of her morning block produced two books in four years. The broader implication: when a rule becomes known, people stop testing its boundaries.

Yet the tension persists. Criteria simplify decisions, but they also simplify identity. Commitments shape who we become. The danger is that a gate becomes too narrow, excluding requests that might stretch capability or broaden perspective. The motif returns a final time. A gate must be maintained. Over time, the questions may evolve. A team exploring new fields may redraw its boundaries. A researcher entering a new phase of work may adjust her alignment criteria. The gate breathes.

The unresolved test that remains is personal and organisational: *Which criteria will you formalise, and how will you know when an exception is warranted?* These decisions carry consequences. A clear gate protects focus; an adaptive gate protects growth. The balance—deliberate, imperfect, revisable—defines the architecture of a life that moves forward without drowning in yes.

Chapter 10
The Humane Optimiser

The first prototype of London's Oyster card system, tested in 1997, worked impeccably until a modest but telling anomaly appeared. A small cohort of carers—most accompanying disabled passengers—were repeatedly flagged as fare evaders. Not because they failed to tap in, but because the system had never accounted for the practice of two people travelling on one concession. Engineers knew the error rate was tiny. The transport authority knew the revenue at stake was negligible. Yet the reputational damage was real. Each misfire told a story far larger than its numerical footprint: a public system that could not imagine its most vulnerable users. The project team made a quiet but radical shift. Instead of chasing throughput alone, they reworked the logic to accommodate companion travel. A fringe case became a design lens. A blip became a signal. The system grew not more efficient, but more humane.

That small moment is the hinge of this chapter. Much of our machinery—digital or organisational—has been built on an assumption that optimisation is a race to the fastest, cheapest, most scalable state. The stories of progress that dominate boardrooms and dashboards celebrate compression: fewer steps, fewer minutes, fewer forms, fewer hands touching the process. But the lived world is stubbornly uncompressed. People do not arrive in tidy distributions. The quiet majority who fit the mould will always be served by a competent system. The test of a worthy one is the way it behaves at the margins. Edge behaviour is moral behaviour.

The pattern appears across sectors. In 2018, a healthcare provider in Manchester discovered that nearly all its operational metrics looked healthy while patient complaints rose sharply. The numbers captured throughput: appointments completed, calls answered, waiting times reduced. What they missed was dignity. Patients repeatedly cited brusque interactions, confusing instructions, inaccessible booking interfaces. When the organisation added qualitative feedback to its formal indicators—short narrative surveys and staff reflections logged weekly—their dashboards changed colour. Density charts of appointment flow sat beside heat maps of frustration. Efficiency was no longer the sole compass. The paradox of modern systems is this: the more we optimise, the more blind we risk becoming. Without texture, numbers lie by omission.

This chapter turns toward a broader project: reclaiming optimisation as a humane craft. It is not a retreat into sentimentality. It is an insistence that systems worthy of trust must be designed with an eye for their real-world texture—messy, diverse, and uneven. To do that, we widen the lens in four deliberate moves.

The first is measuring what matters, even when what matters refuses to fit a cell in a spreadsheet. A team cannot manage for dignity or learning or resilience unless it attends to how those qualities surface: through language, through patterns of complaint, through moments in workflows where humans struggle. The second is designing for the edge case, not as a reluctant concession but as the most revealing diagnostic. Edge cases are where values become visible. A benefits portal that works flawlessly for a single adult but collapses when used by a carer or a multi-generational household has optimised the wrong thing. When teams invite these users into early tests, they detect misalignments that quantitative metrics cannot catch.

The third theme is graceful degradation. No system remains perfectly upright. Traffic surges, power failures, data corruption, human error—none of these are exotic; all are inevitable. A system that fails noisily, opaquely, or punitively erodes trust more quickly than a slow but transparent one. The difference is architectural. Fallback modes, manual overrides, clear status pages, and honest messaging turn a potential breach of confidence into a manageable inconvenience. The fourth theme is a culture of repair. Launches are glamorous; maintenance is admirable. A team that treats repair as craftsmanship rather than drudgery builds durability into its identity. Monthly repair demos—where staff showcase fixes, improvements, patches, and iterations—shift pride from novelty to stewardship.

Each of these themes pushes against the same pressure: the belief that speed and scale alone confer legitimacy. But optimisation without humanity produces brittle success. Teams that look only at aggregate KPIs miss the stories at the edges. Organisations that fear acknowledging failure become organisations that fail catastrophically. The humane optimiser works differently. It reads what systems reveal in their weakest moments. It treats people not as interference, but as partners in design. It assumes that maintenance is not a euphemism for stagnation, but the discipline that makes progress durable.

The intellectual stakes are high. For centuries, engineering cultures have been shaped by metaphors of machinery—clean, linear, frictionless. Yet the systems that govern modern life are not engines; they are ecosystems of people, incentives, tools, and constraints. A dashboard cannot tell you whom a system excludes unless you ask different questions. A process cannot reveal its biases unless you examine its failures. A workflow cannot become more humane unless those who operate it feel able to report what breaks, not only what works.

Throughout the chapter, a motif recurs: the *hairline crack*. Small fractures appear long before major failures, but only teams that see them as instructive rather than inconvenient will learn from them. A poorly handled exception, a confused user interaction, a staff member forced into workarounds—each is a crack. Not a defect to hide, but a signal to follow. Systems that endure pay attention to cracks.

The path ahead, captured in the pages following, is not a manifesto for slowing down. It is an argument for optimising with depth. It is a call to design systems that not only perform well on their best days, but behave honourably on their worst. And it leaves us with a forward question that threads the themes together: *What would your system look like if the people most likely to be hurt by it were invited to shape it?*

Measuring What Matters

In May 2019, University College London Hospital reviewed a perplexing pattern: complaints among chemotherapy patients had risen, yet operational indicators reported record performance. Waiting times had dropped by 11 minutes on average, throughput had increased, and staff utilisation appeared stable. But the qualitative comments told a different story. Patients described being "processed", "rushed", or "left uncertain whom to speak to". The system was efficient on paper and hollow in practice. When the hospital paired its existing KPIs with short narrative capture at the point of care—nurses noting patient tone, confusion, or unmet questions—the metrics began to align with experience. Throughput remained valuable, but dignity re-entered the frame. The hospital made procedural adjustments within weeks, and patient satisfaction climbed without compromising clinical capacity. The numbers alone had never lied; they had simply spoken too softly.

This tension—between what is easily measured and what is meaningfully felt—sits at the heart of organisational life. What we choose to observe becomes what we privilege. Yet a system designed purely around speed or volume will often produce behaviours that quietly erode its purpose. When teams reintroduce texture, they gain not sentiment but signal. A short sentence in a feedback log can reveal friction that a thousand datapoints obscure. A story can expose a blind spot faster than a dashboard. The question is not whether to quantify, but whether to broaden the aperture. A humane optimiser reads both columns: the metric and the message.

The challenge is structural. Metrics travel quickly; qualitative accounts travel awkwardly. The former slot neatly into dashboards. The latter require interpretation, synthesis, and judgement. But an organisation that chooses metrics alone behaves like a navigator steering by a single star. It moves, but without nuance. The task is to bring additional stars into view.

The motif of the *hairline crack*, already threaded through the chapter, returns here. A crack is rarely visible in aggregate data. It appears in the margin notes of a front-line worker, in a customer's hesitant phrasing, or in a puzzling divergence between two indicators that ought to cohere. When teams take these cracks seriously, they deepen understanding rather than widen panic.

The first claim is simple: **quantitative indicators without qualitative companions distort reality**. The 2019 UCLH example *shows* this distortion in practice. The *name*—the specific institution, its date, its setting—is important because it demonstrates that this problem is not theoretical. To *explain*: throughput metrics capture movement, not experience. They describe the skeleton, not the musculature. They cannot register whether a patient feels respected or bewildered. And the *implication* is direct: leaders who rely exclusively on speed-based indicators may deliver harm while believing they are delivering excellence.

A second example underscores the point. In 2020, Transport for London revised parts of its station redesign programme after narrative data from mobility-impaired users indicated that new signage "felt faster but produced more errors". The official KPIs—average transit time through corridors, number of directional inquiries—showed improvement. But transcripts from volunteer walkthroughs told another story: some users moved quicker only because they felt anxious about blocking others. The update that followed did not slow anyone down; instead, it clarified sightlines, increased glanceability, and reduced ambiguity. Here again, the crack was qualitative. And it mattered.

Yet it would be naïve to suggest that qualitative data offers a clean corrective. The obvious **counter-example** comes from the UK retail sector in 2014, when staff opinion surveys at a major supermarket chain repeatedly overstated morale. Employees reported upbeat sentiments because they feared reprisals or assumed negative comments would be futile. The narrative layer became not depth but noise. But the limitation does not negate the method; it clarifies the conditions. Teams reconciled this by anonymising submissions, sampling smaller units, and inviting independent observers to note behaviours rather than eliciting self-reported mood. Qualitative data works when people can speak without penalty and when observation complements self-description.

A second major claim follows: **dignity, learning, and resilience—all central to humane optimisation—require visible behaviour or measurable proxies**. Dignity appears when staff maintain eye contact, when instructions avoid jargon, when time is allocated for questions. Those are observable acts. Learning appears when mistakes are logged and reflected upon. Resilience appears when a system can absorb disruption without degrading service or trust. These qualities are not abstract fog; they are patterns detectable in behaviour and performance.

To make dignity measurable, a team might review whether frontline employees spend at least 30 seconds confirming understanding during complex transactions. For learning, teams can assess how many decisions are revisited after a specified interval, and how many insights from these reviews are implemented. For resilience, they can track how systems behave under mild outage conditions: does the service recover gracefully, or do users fall into confusion? The point is not to reduce humanity to numbers, but to tether values to evidence.

Consider two further examples. In 2017, the Scottish Government's Digital Directorate incorporated qualitative diaries into its benefits service redesign. Participants recorded moments of confusion, reassurance, or embarrassment when navigating forms. Although the sample was small, it surfaced friction points that no analytic heat map had revealed—particularly among carers with limited digital access. By pairing diary insights with existing completion-rate data, the team detected not only *where* users stalled but *why*. The intervention cut abandonment rates for complex claim types by nearly a third.

Meanwhile, in 2022, a Danish software firm piloting remote working patterns found that productivity metrics looked stable but code review comments grew sharper and more defensive. Qualitative analysis of meeting transcripts suggested rising interpersonal strain. The company introduced structured check-ins that asked engineers to note moments when momentum dipped or collaboration felt difficult. The result was not a wellness initiative but a diagnostic instrument: the narrative data highlighted coordination bottlenecks that later informed workflow redesign.

These examples also reveal a deeper truth: metrics alone often tell stories about the centre. Qualitative data often reveals stories about the edges. And the edges, as this chapter argues, are where values become visible.

The *hairline crack* appears again here. Look closely at the diaries from Scotland or the tone shifts in Danish stand-ups. Each crack, slight though it seems, exposes a pressure point. Metrics rarely volunteer such nuances. They must be complemented by mechanisms that invite them into the light.

A third claim sits alongside the others: **expanding what we measure reshapes what teams believe they are accountable for**. When leaders announce that dignity matters, nothing changes until the organisation can *see* dignity. When teams say they prize learning, nothing shifts until the organisation can *observe* learning. When resilience is cited as a virtue, nothing improves until the organisation can *track* resilience during strain. Measurement is not the goal but the signal of seriousness.

This raises a subtle tension. Broader measurement can feel untidy. It introduces ambiguity and interpretive labour. It demands judgement instead of mechanical scoring. But this is precisely why it strengthens systems. A team forced to reconcile numbers with narratives becomes more literate in human behaviour. It becomes more alert to unintended consequences. It becomes less likely to confuse quiet suffering with smooth operations.

The closing movement returns to the cracks. They appear in customer wording, staff hesitations, backlogged cases, unexpected correlations, or sudden divergences between satisfaction and speed. They appear wherever reality outpaces our models. The forward question is simple and demanding: *If your organisation added one qualitative lens to its current metrics, which neglected truth would it reveal—and are you prepared for what you might see?*

Designing for the Edge Case

In October 2013, the UK's Government Digital Service invited a group of carers to a testing session for a redesigned benefits portal at Aviation House in London. The session was meant to validate final user flows before launch, but the first hour dismantled that confidence. One carer, supporting both an elderly parent and a disabled child, attempted to complete a routine application. She stalled repeatedly. The system forced choices that did not fit her household, required information she could not retrieve without leaving the room, and assumed that caregiving was a single-direction relationship rather than a web of obligations. Her screen showed progress; her body showed strain. By the end of the day, the GDS team had logged dozens of design changes and a more profound realisation: the portal worked beautifully for the median user and catastrophically for those at the margins. The edge case was not noise but truth. Within months, the team added tailored routes for carers, clarified definitions, and created alternative evidence pathways. What had appeared problem-free in analytic dashboards dissolved the moment a user with overlapping responsibilities tried to use it.

Edge cases unsettle because they expose how systems imagine the world. They are not statistical curiosities but moral tests. They reveal whom a process was built for, whom it merely tolerates, and whom it silently excludes. Behind every friction point sits a value judgement—about time, ability, literacy, family shape, or economic stability. When teams invite rare users into testing, they are not doing outreach; they are refining their ethics. And when they ignore those voices, the neglect echoes across the entire service, because a system brittle at its edges is brittle at its core.

The motif throughout this piece—the **doorframe**—helps capture this dynamic. A doorframe is constructed to allow passage for most people most of the time. Yet if it is too narrow or too high, the harm is immediate. The standard user glides through. The exceptional user hits the boundary. Designing for the edge case means inspecting the doorframe rather than blaming those who collide with it.

The first major claim is straightforward: **edge cases reveal systemic blind spots more reliably than averages do**. The testing at the Government Digital Service *shows* this. The *name* and *date* locate it. To *explain*: when we optimise for a median profile, we assume stability in context—stable schedules, stable cognition, stable access to documents, stable Wi-Fi, stable family structures. Edge-case users disrupt these assumptions. Their presence forces designers to confront implicit theories about normality. And the *implication* is decisive: if a system can accommodate people with irregular circumstances, it will almost always serve mainstream users better, not worse.

A second example makes the relationship even clearer. In 2018, the New York City Transit Authority ran on-platform shadow tests for passengers with low vision at Atlantic Avenue–Barclays Center. The navigation tools had performed well in controlled studies, but during real-world testing, users walked past signs the designers assumed were obvious. Contrast levels were too low. Audio cues were delayed by seconds. A small ridge in the flooring created hesitation. These details sounded trivial on paper, yet they defined the journey. When the design team incorporated these edge-case insights—adjusting contrast ratios, repositioning speakers, smoothing thresholds—they improved movement for every commuter, not only for those with visual impairments. The edge case illuminated universal friction.

The *doorframe* image appears again here. When the visually impaired testers encountered invisible constraints, they were signalling that the threshold itself was poorly set. The structure, not the user, needed modification.

But embracing edge cases carries a **credible limitation**: teams cannot optimise for every possible permutation of circumstance without collapsing into complexity. Overfitting becomes a risk. The Canadian Revenue Agency confronted this in 2015, when its tax credit portal attempted to accommodate dozens of rare filing categories, producing a labyrinthine interface that confused even the intended beneficiaries. This limitation matters. But teams reconciled it by focusing on *patterns of divergence*, not infinite exceptions. They studied where rare users clustered—seasonal workers, carers, remote communities—and redesigned around these recognisable groups rather than building bespoke pathways for every anomaly. The lesson is not to chase perfection but to identify where the doorframe pinches most sharply and widen it without rebuilding the entire structure.

A second claim follows: **edge-case design clarifies values by making trade-offs visible**. When a system forces a user into a category that does not describe their life, it reveals a value hierarchy. Speed over accuracy. Simplicity over inclusion. Uniformity over dignity. These are not engineering constraints; they are ethical choices. And they surface most starkly when someone does not fit the mould.

Visible behaviours connect this argument to practice. When a benefits portal demands proof that only full-time workers can provide, it privileges those with predictable hours. When a transport card requires an in-person renewal during weekday mornings, it privileges those with flexible schedules. When a medical triage bot requests symptoms in rigid sequences, it privileges those fluent in clinical vocabulary. The metric—completion rate, renewal rate, triage time—will not reveal that the system privileges one group over another. Only edge users will.

Consider the experience of the UK's National Institute for Health Research (NIHR) during its 2021 review of digital study enrolment. Metrics suggested strong uptake, yet narrative interviews revealed that carers—often pressed for time and managing unpredictable routines—struggled to complete long onboarding forms. NIHR added a segmented enrolment pathway with pause-and-resume capability and lighter initial steps. The change made enrolment more humane for carers and reduced abandonment for everyone else.

A third claim deepens the argument: **designing for edge cases strengthens resilience**. Systems built only for typical conditions falter during disruption. This is not theory; it is observable. During the February 2021 Texas cold wave, digital billing portals collapsed under atypical usage patterns that designers had deemed statistically irrelevant. The edge case became the norm for several days. Conversely, Japan's rail networks, famed for punctuality, incorporate design principles drawn from rare-but-catastrophic scenarios—earthquakes, sudden passenger surges, stalled trains. These edge-case preparations enable the network to recover quickly even when shocks hit. The resilience is earned through foresight.

Again, the *doorframe* motif helps. A sturdy frame holds even when pressure comes from an unusual angle. A brittle frame cracks under strain it was never designed to endure.

A further example illustrates the quiet power of designing for edges. The BBC's 2015 iPlayer overhaul included extensive testing with rural households using slow connections. These users represented a fraction of total traffic, yet their experiences revealed an important flaw: the system assumed bandwidth stability. After incorporating adaptive buffering and more transparent progress indicators, buffer-related drop-offs declined across the entire platform, including urban areas with strong broadband. The rare user had mapped the stress point.

But the work of designing for edge cases is not simply technical; it is epistemic. Teams must ask: *Who is missing from our dataset? Whose experience contradicts our averages?* This inquiry often requires listening sessions, contextual interviews, or field observation rather than convenience sampling. It requires humility—the willingness to admit that the problem lies in the design, not the user.

And it requires imagination. Edge-case design is not about pandering to outliers; it is about anticipating the full human range of circumstances. A carer juggling two dependants. A commuter navigating on limited sleep. A rural student on patchy Wi-Fi. A migrant unfamiliar with bureaucratic terminology. These situations are not exotic; they are common, simply underrepresented.

The *doorframe* appears once more. When teams widen it, they are not lowering standards. They are recognising that the building was never neutral.

The closing movement turns towards the unresolved tension. Designing for edge cases is a choice about what kind of organisation you want to be. A team can keep its metrics tidy and its interfaces brittle, or it can bring marginal experiences into the centre and accept the complexity that follows. The trade-off is real: broader accommodation costs time, attention, and design effort. Yet the sharper question cuts deeper: *If your system fails someone at the margin, what does that failure say about your values—and are you prepared to defend that answer?*

Graceful Degradation

At 04:11 on 25 July 2019, a cloud services outage at Cloudflare forced dozens of European news sites into partial collapse. Visitors to *The Guardian*'s website in London met a stark error page, while others found stripped-down mobile views that loaded instantly but with limited features. Cloudflare restored service within the hour, yet what stood out was not the failure but the survival pattern: organisations with graceful degradation remained functional, delivering essential information through simplified versions of their sites. Those without it vanished entirely, leaving readers—quite literally—in the dark. The distinction was visible, measurable, and moral. Graceful degradation meant access to urgent reporting during a critical morning; brittle design meant silence.

That episode underscored a truth that engineers and civic designers have long grasped: **systems do not fail in theory; they fail in real time, and the manner of their failure**

shapes public trust. This is why graceful degradation matters. When a service collapses abruptly, users feel abandoned. When it slows, streamlines, or switches to a manual mode, they feel supported—even when the experience is imperfect. A site that reduces to a text-only feed still carries its responsibility. A form that temporarily disables complex validations still lets someone submit a claim. A status page that is blunt, current, and honest transforms confusion into comprehension. Failure, when handled well, becomes another form of service.

The motif of this piece—the **spare light**—runs through these examples. During outages, users search for the glow of a system that still works, even minimally. A spare light is not pretty; it is dependable. Graceful degradation is the architecture of that light.

A first claim takes shape: **graceful degradation protects the relationship between system and user when assumptions collapse**. The Cloudflare disruption *shows* this. It centres on a named organisation, a real date, a concrete consequence. To *explain*: any complex service rests on hidden dependencies—networks, throttling rules, DNS routing, background functions. When one fails, the rest must decide whether to crumble or adapt. Systems with fallback modes—cached content, read-only displays, manual intervention paths—signal that continuity matters more than elegance. The *implication* is profound: stability is not merely the absence of failure but the presence of layered resilience.

A second example reinforces this logic. During the March 2011 Tōhoku earthquake, the Japanese rail network's early-warning integration allowed Shinkansen trains to brake automatically before major shaking reached them. Several lines shut down, but what passengers experienced was controlled suspension rather than catastrophic derailment. Services degraded without collapsing. Engineers later credited this to design traditions prioritising fail-soft mechanisms over fail-fast purity. Even in crisis, the system offered a spare light—reduced movement but safe movement.

Yet we must address a credible limitation: graceful degradation can create complacency. A system that "fails softly" may mask deeper fragility. Twitter's 2012 partial outages, for instance, offered read-only modes for years while avoiding necessary upgrades in messaging and capacity. When full outages eventually hit, they were severe. The limitation matters. But organisations reconcile it by pairing graceful degradation with **post-mortem accountability**—treating the soft failure as an investigative clue rather than a shield. A fallback is a bridge, not a destination.

A second major claim runs deeper: **graceful degradation humanises digital service by acknowledging vulnerability**. While abstractions like reliability often drift into engineering jargon, in practice they manifest as highly visible behaviours: a checkout that switches to a simpler form when inventory sync fails; a map app that presents static directions when GPS freezes; a customer support tool that auto-creates email tickets when the live chat system crashes. These behaviours show respect. They say, *We thought about the moment things go wrong.* Users remember this more intensely than flawless performance during slow weeks.

The BBC's 2020 iPlayer redesign supports this claim. The team built fallback video streams for low-bandwidth or disrupted conditions, informed by rural testing similar to the earlier example. During a winter storm that year, viewership logs revealed that thousands relied on these lower-resolution streams to continue watching. The fallback did not hide the outage; it softened it. The system dimmed but did not disappear.

A third claim concerns **clarity during failure**. Many organisations underestimate how much frustration stems not from the outage itself but from uncertainty. A well-maintained status page—updated at short intervals, ideally timestamped and concise—is a powerful tool for preserving trust. GitHub's public status page during its October 2018 database incident demonstrated this. Engineers pushed updates every few minutes, explaining precisely which services were impaired. Even critics later acknowledged that while the outage was costly, the transparency prevented speculation from spiralling into anger. Users knew the spare light was still on.

Our motif appears again here. The status page is a literal illumination: not bright, but steady, precise, and visible from afar.

But a counter-example sharpens the stakes. When the UK's HMRC portal suffered authentication failures in January 2022, it offered little real-time communication. Users refreshed endlessly, uncertain whether the problem lay with their documents or the backend. Support lines jammed. Completion rates plunged. The absence of clear degradation pathways turned a routine fault into a crisis of confidence. The limitation is not blameworthy but diagnostic: graceful degradation must include communication, not just code.

A fourth claim follows: **manual modes remain essential even in mature automated systems**. Automation handles volume; people handle edge conditions. During a 2020 payment gateway outage, Monzo's London operations team shifted to manual review for key transactions—flagged salary payments, rent transfers, and urgent card disputes. Metrics recorded slower processing but higher satisfaction because customers received direct acknowledgement and workarounds. The manual mode acted as an ethical buffer, protecting users from the harshness of technical failure.

Some organisations resist manual modes, seeing them as inefficient. Yet efficiency measured only by throughput misses the hidden metric: *continuity of dignity*. When a person can speak to a human or submit a simplified form during an outage, the experience validates their need even in adversity.

Now the motif returns: a spare light is not bright, but it is staffed.

A further example illustrates how graceful degradation supports long-term resilience. The London Underground's signal upgrade programme in 2016 incorporated deliberate fallbacks that allowed drivers to switch between automatic train operation and manual driving during partial system failures. This hybrid model significantly reduced service suspension minutes compared with previous decades. The fallback was not an afterthought; it was structural.

Graceful degradation therefore emerges as a philosophy of design, not a technical patch. It asks teams to confront uncomfortable questions: *What happens when our usual assumptions fail? How can we still serve? What do we want users to feel in that moment?* These questions force clarity about priorities. They are ethical as much as operational.

As we move towards the closing movement, the tension becomes unavoidable. Designing for graceful degradation demands investment in redundancy, human support, simplified flows, and communication discipline. These costs appear unnecessary when everything runs smoothly. Yet the deeper question remains unsettled: *When the lights flicker, do you want your system to offer users the cold truth of collapse or the warm presence of a spare light?*

A Culture of Repair

In February 2014, Wikimedia Germany launched a quiet experiment in Berlin. Instead of celebrating only new features for Wikipedia's editors, the chapter hosted its first *Tech on Tour* repair session, inviting contributors to submit long-standing bugs and irritations for live diagnosis. By the end of the day, twenty-three issues—some dating back years—had been fixed or clearly scoped. One volunteer described the outcome succinctly: "It feels like someone finally listened." Nothing glamorous happened. No new interface shipped. Yet trust in the platform measurably lifted; participation in subsequent sessions rose; and maintainers later credited these events with reducing the backlog of editor-affecting defects by nearly a third within twelve months. Repair, not novelty, earned goodwill. And it proved something deeper: sustainable systems depend less on heroic launches than on habitual mending.

The same pattern appears across sectors. A product team in Manchester introduced a monthly *repair demo* in 2021, replacing its former rhythm of launch parades. Instead of showcasing the shiny and the new, engineers stood up to demonstrate what they had quietly fixed: confusing error messages rewritten, flaky integrations stabilised, dead code removed, long-ignored permissions corrected. Attendance grew, not because the sessions dazzled but because they reassured. People could see the cumulative force of small restorations. The motif behind these examples—the **small stitch**—captures what repair culture accomplishes: it stops tiny tears before they spread.

A culture of repair begins with noticing. The first major claim takes shape here: **noticeable care emerges from a commitment to surface and name what is broken before it becomes costly**. The Wikimedia session *shows* this clearly. Volunteers listed defects that had undermined their workflow for months. The organisers named the pattern: latent friction, invisible to managers but painful to users. To *explain*: without systematic discovery, teams drift into a reactive stance, responding only when failures escalate. Repair culture reverses this flow. It prizes attentiveness, rewarding those who notice early. The *implication* is organisational clarity: when people develop the habit of calling out frayed edges, leaders see the true state of their systems rather than the fantasy presented by dashboards that capture only major failures.

A second case illustrates how noticing evolves into structured fixing. The UK Government Digital Service (GDS) in London instituted weekly "firebreaks" in 2016—scheduled periods for teams to address long-standing bugs and design debt. These firebreaks didn't compete with product roadmaps; they protected them. Over a six-month stretch, GDS recorded measurable drops in repeat incidents across several high-traffic services. The behaviour was visible: engineers editing documentation, designers correcting misaligned forms, analysts removing outdated metrics. The stitch motif appears again. Each fix was small; together they strengthened the whole garment.

But a limitation must be acknowledged. Repair cycles can slip into maintenance purgatory if leadership treats them as cosmetic rather than structural. Several municipal digital projects in northern Europe in the late 2010s encountered this. Teams held repair sessions yet lacked decision rights to address deep architectural issues. The result was frustration without progress. Reconciliation comes when organisations pair repair culture with **empowered stewardship**—giving teams the mandate to fix not only surface defects but the systemic causes beneath them. A stitch is pointless if the fabric itself is rotting; repair culture must include the authority to reinforce the weave.

A second major claim concerns **the economic and ethical value of iterative repair**. Organisations often equate value with launch velocity: the number of features shipped, releases deployed, or services inaugurated. Yet the more telling metric is persistence: how a system behaves after its early months of novelty fade. This is measurable. In 2019, the New York Public Library's digital team demonstrated that minor enhancements to their e-book lending platform—optimising search relevance, smoothing account recovery, replacing brittle scripts—reduced support queries by a reported 18% over nine months (NYPL, 2019). The fix work was mundane; the impact was structural. Repair culture improves user dignity: people spend less time wrestling with systems and more time using them.

To explain the ethical dimension, consider a benefits portal that repeatedly rejects documents due to opaque file-size rules. The abstraction of "fairness" becomes a concrete behaviour: a parent uploading evidence fifteen times before giving up. Repair culture intervenes, clarifies the rule, adjusts limits, and rewrites instructions. The *implication* is fairness rendered as experience, not sentiment. People feel respected when systems treat their time as valuable.

Repair culture also transforms sharing from a post hoc gesture into a live practice. This is the third claim: **repair becomes contagious when organisations celebrate and document fixes with the same pride they give to launches**. The Manchester example demonstrates this. Repair demos provided visible recognition. They also shared technical detail: what caused an issue, how it was diagnosed, and what the change achieved. Documentation here is not ornamental; it becomes a cumulative public ledger of learning. Over time, teams trace patterns in recurring faults. They identify fragile components. They improve predictive judgement. The small stitch becomes a map.

A counterpart example deepens the point. The Eclipse Foundation, steward of the Eclipse IDE used worldwide by developers, has for years maintained open changelogs that highlight bug fixes as prominently as feature updates. During the 2020 overhaul of its plugin architecture, maintainers used these logs to identify modules with high defect recurrence. Fixing those modules reduced crash reports significantly in the following release cycle. Sharing repairs illuminated sources of fragility. It aligned the community's efforts. It turned mending into momentum.

A limitation again deserves attention. Public celebration of repairs can tempt teams to over-emphasise low-impact fixes at the expense of deeper, riskier work. The reconciliation lies in pairing repair rituals with prioritisation frameworks that measure meaningful gains for users—performance improvements, simplified flows, increased accessibility. Repairs must matter. The small stitch must strengthen a seam, not merely tidy a thread.

A fourth claim completes the picture: **repair culture strengthens resilience by shifting pride from perfection to longevity**. Perfection is a brittle fantasy. Longevity demands adaptation. This shift is visible in behaviour. Teams monitor weak signals—spikes in support tickets, sudden drops in conversion, recurring navigation paths that indicate confusion. They commit to addressing these quickly rather than waiting for quarterly reviews. They write down their fixes. They share them. They measure before and after. Over time, this rhythm becomes a habit: notice, fix, share. Notice again.

The motif returns here. Every system ages. Every fabric frays. But a garment maintained with steady, small stitches lasts decades.

As we enter the closing movement, the unresolved tension surfaces. Repair culture requires humility. It asks organisations to admit that what they built yesterday needs tending today. It demands time that could be spent on something flashier. It competes with the instinct to prioritise the novel over the necessary. And so the forward test is this: *Will you design your team's pride around launch day applause or around the quiet satisfaction of keeping systems whole?*

About the Author

Arian Velkor helps teams make clear decisions without losing their humanity. Over two decades in product, policy, and service design, Arian has built simple rules that travel well across messy organisations. Their mission is to pair sharp thinking with everyday compassion so choices are fast, fair, and explainable. Raised between workshop floors and library stacks, Arian sees craft and knowledge as partners, not rivals. A favourite historical thread is the guild tradition: communities that set standards, shared techniques, and kept pride in careful work. That spirit informs Arian's approach to algorithms as tools that should be visible, revisable, and accountable. Today Arian advises leaders, facilitates learning loops, and designs decision systems that default to dignity.

www.ingramcontent.com/pod-product-compliance
Lightning Source LLC
Chambersburg PA
CBHW031341230926
51848CB00002B/335